TO A MOUNTAIN IN TIBET

COLIN THUBRON

———

To a
Mountain
in
Tibet

HARPER PERENNIAL

NEW YORK • LONDON • TORONTO • SYDNEY • NEW DELHI • AUCKLAND

HARPER ● PERENNIAL

First published in Great Britain in 2010 by Chatto & Windus, an imprint of Random House Group Ltd.

First U.S. hardcover published in 2011 by HarperCollins Publishers.

P.S.™ is a trademark of HarperCollins Publishers.

HarperCollins books may be purchased for educational, business, or sales promotional use. For information please write: Special Markets Department, HarperCollins Publishers, 10 East 53rd Street, New York, NY 10022.

FIRST HARPER PERENNIAL EDITION PUBLISHED 2012.

Library of Congress Cataloging-in-Publication Data has been applied for.

ISBN 978-0-06-176827-9 (pbk.)

12 13 14 15 16 OFF/RRD 10 9 8 7 6 5 4 3 2 1

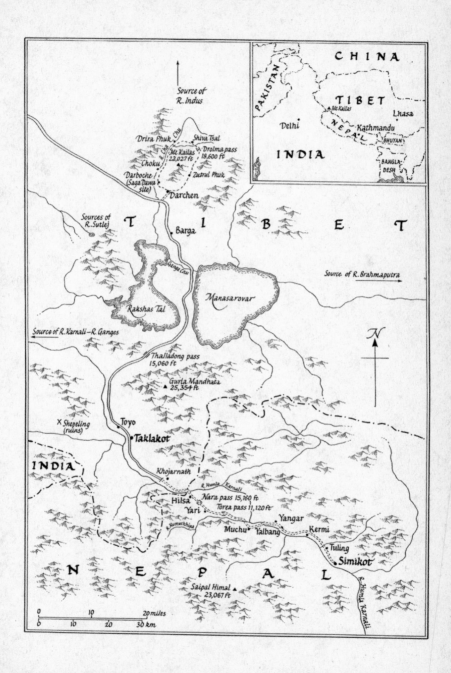

TO A MOUNTAIN IN TIBET

CHAPTER ONE
· · · · · · ·

The sun is rising to its zenith. Silver-grey boulders lie tumbled along the track among mattresses of thorns and smoke-blue flowers. The storm clouds that hang on the farther mountains do not move. There is no sound but the scrunch of our boots and the clink of the sherpa's trekking pole. Underfoot the stones glisten with quartz.

These first hours have a raw exhilaration. The track shimmers ahead with a hard brilliance. The earth is young again. Perhaps it is the altitude that brings this lightness and anticipation. Within an hour we have flown from near sea level to over 8,000 feet, and I feel weightless, as if my steps will leave no trace.

Beneath us the little town of Simikot hangs above an abyss of empty valleys. Its corrugated-iron roofs flash among patches of green barley. It is slipping behind us. From its runway of parched earth the Twin Otter aircraft that carried us in has already turned and flown away between the mountains. There are no roads here. Humla is the remotest region in Nepal, little visited by trekkers even now. The nearest paved highway – the lowland route from Kathmandu to Delhi – lies hundreds of mountain miles to the south, and to the east the climbers' lodestars – Dhaulagiri, Annapurna, Everest – are out of sight.

As we walk, a dark-forested gully opens to the west, carving a giant corridor through the mountains. Its walls rise in vertiginous foothills towards 15,000-foot summits gashed with snow and clouds. Noiselessly far below us, through this immense gulf so steep as often to lie out of sight, the Karnali river is raging coldly down from the highest source of the Ganges. It is nowhere navigable, but for the next ten days it will steer us northwards. It twists ahead with a chill magnetism, mounting by icy steps higher and deeper through the western Himalaya, for a hundred miles before us, into Tibet.

By trekkers' standards our party is small and swift: a guide, a cook, a horse man, myself. We move scattered above the river, while lone traders pass us the other way, leading their stocky horse and mule trains between lonely villages. They are dark, slight men in torn anoraks and brimless headgear, marching to the clank of their animals' tin bells and crying softly to the strays to keep in line. Their women walk alongside, sashed and scarved in magenta and blue, their sinewy wrists layered in bracelets, their nostrils and ears dangling golden discs. They look fierce and open, and laughingly meet your eyes. The delicacy of the plains has gone.

We reach a cairn stuck with weathered stakes, then descend through pines towards the river. Its noise rises to us in the hiss of far-down cataracts. Peacefully beneath us, and seaming the far banks in long yellow shelves, the terraces of an unseen village are ripening with corn. The slopes flame with the reds and purples of late spring, with shrubs I do not know. Giant walnut trees appear, and silvery aromatic shrubs, while overhead the mountain peaks gather in jagged crenellations and seem to enclose the place in a private peace.

We are through the village almost without knowing. Granite boulders overshadow dwellings frailer than they: cottages of dry-stone walls and bleached timbers sunk among the igneous rocks. They look half deserted, mellow and pastoral above their fields, so that as we go on high above the river, past rice paddies and a little shrine to Shiva, I imagine this a valley of Arcadian quiet.

Then a man joins us on the path. He is vivid with troubles. His jacket is patched, his trainers split. He fires a volley of questions at the sherpa. How can he get out of this place? There's nothing for anybody here. His family can't support itself on its patch of rice field . . . it isn't enough . . .

His eyes spear us out of a sun-blackened face. He follows us for miles. He cannot bear to let us go: we, who carry the aura of a wider world. He has never been to Kathmandu, never left this region. But rain has loosened the earth around his house, and it is sliding down towards the river.

'I am fifty-six now . . . my life is too poor . . . My son and daughter-in-law want to buy a new horse, but we cannot afford one . . . a horse is forty thousand rupees . . .'

Yet this dirge comes with a hardy sparkle, as if he were talking about other people. He grins with disordered teeth. 'Their horse is old . . . it will die . . .'

Of course. This is a cruel region in a poverty-stricken land: bitter winters and narrow, rock-strewn earth. Arcadia is falling to bits as he speaks. The farmed terraces are dropping behind, and above us the naked rock is bursting through the green hillsides in huge, serrated shoulders.

Sometimes the track lifts precipitously on steps hewn sheer from the cliff face, or ascends on rubble stairways where a stumble will pitch us into the abyss.

At one of these bottlenecks we find the rock daubed red with the Maoist rebel emblem – a hammer-and-sickle circled beside a swastika (here an archaic symbol of good fortune) – but the guerrillas themselves have gone. For ten years they paralysed this region, and would politely leach for money the few foreigners who ventured in. They took over 13,000 Nepalese lives. But now, three years later, with Kathmandu's royal dynasty swept away, they are jostling for power with the decrepit politicians in the capital, and their old slogan – 'Follow the Maoist path!' – is flaking from cliffs and walls.

At last the farmer turns back, waving buoyantly, his voice fading among the rocks. 'We have no king now . . . we have nothing . . .' And then, as if, after all, he might follow us to the end: 'Where are you going?'

When the sherpa cries back, 'Mount Kailas!' the name echoes down the river like a broken secret. The farmer does not hear it. It is the noise of somewhere imagined or hopelessly far away.

And so, in the West, it still seems. The most sacred of the world's mountains – holy to one fifth of the earth's people – remains withdrawn on its plateau like a pious illusion. For years I had heard of it only as a figment. Isolated beyond the parapet of the central Himalaya, it permeated early Hindu scriptures as the mystic Mount Meru, whose origins go back to the dawn of Aryan time. In this incarnation it rotates like a spindle at the axis of all creation, ascending immeasurable miles to the palace of Brahma, greatest and most remote of the gods, and plunging as deep beneath the earth. From its foot flow the four rivers that nourish the world, and everything created – trees, rocks, humans – finds its blueprint here. In time the mystical Meru and the earthly Kailas merged in people's minds. Early wanderers to the source of the four great Indian rivers – the Indus, the Ganges, the Sutlej and the Brahmaputra – found to their wonder that each one rose near a cardinal point of Kailas.

So people discovered the heart of the world. It was a site of astral beauty, separated from its companion Himalayas as if by divine intent. To the pious, the mountain radiates gold or refracts like crystal. It is the source of the universe, created from cosmic waters and the mind of Brahma, who is yet himself mortal and will pass away. The sun and the planets orbit it. The Pole Star hangs immutable above. The continents of the world radiate from its centre like lotus petals on a precious sea (humans occupy the southern petal) and its slopes are heady with the gardens of paradise.

But the God of Death dwells on the mountain. Nothing is total, nothing permanent – not even he. All is flux. In the oceans around Kailas-Meru, beyond a ring of iron mountains, countless embodiments of Meru, each identical to the last, multiply and repeat themselves, dying and resurrecting into eternity.

Around me in the Karnali valley, nothing yet disturbs these dreams. The infant Ganges steepens and roars out of a cleft far on the skyline. The sherpa is trying to sing.

Kailas, I know – the solid, terrestrial peak still invisible ahead – stands in starker terrain than this, stripped of everything but worship. It enters history quickened already by centuries of overlapping divinities. About a millennium ago the pagan gods in charge of the mountain were converted to Buddhism and became its protectors. A few slipped through the net, of course, with even a flying sky goddess, and linger still. But a multitude of Buddhas and bodhisattvas – saints who have delayed their entry into nirvana in order to help others – flew in to occupy the high crags and summits, lighting up the mountain with their compassion. Then the Buddha himself arrived and nailed Kailas to earth with his footprints before it could be carted off by a demon.

The mountain is swathed in such a dense and changing mystique that it eludes simple portrayal. It was on to such a peak that the first Tibetan kings descended from the sky (eventually to be cut off and stranded). Hindus believe its summit to be the palace of Shiva – the lord of destruction and change – who sits there in eternal meditation. But it is unknown when the first pilgrims came. Buddhist herders and Hindu ascetics must have ritually circled the mountain for centuries, and the blessings accruing to them increased marvellously in sacred lore, until it was claimed that a single circuit expunged the sins of a lifetime. The mountain was dangerous to reach, but never quite inaccessible. Only in the nineteenth century did Tibet itself, swayed by a xenophobic China, become a forbidden land. And Kailas kept its own taboos. Its slopes are sacrosanct, and it has never been climbed.

But in recent years it has been protected less by sanctity

than by political intolerance. In 1962, four years before the Cultural Revolution, the Chinese banned all pilgrimage here (although devotees still circled it secretly), and only in 1981 were the first Tibetans and Indians permitted to return. Twelve years later a few trekkers were tentatively allowed to cross the mountain borders between Nepal and Tibet.

My own small journey is one of these. The negotiation of permits – I am entering a military zone – has been fought by an agent in Kathmandu; but the Chinese suspicion of lone travellers compels me to join a group of seven British trekkers on the border – we will separate at the foot of Kailas – for the charade of not entering western Tibet alone. My Nepalese horse man too, a Thakuri from Humla, will leave us at the frontier. But Iswor, my guide, and Ram, the cook, will cross to the mountain with me. They are Tamangs, sturdy people close to the Tibetans, and now they march tactfully behind or ahead of me, their backs piled with over fifty pounds of gear each.

Iswor speaks fractured English. He has the thick shoulders and strong, bandy legs of his people, but at twenty-seven he is young for this job, and shy. Sometimes I imagine a fragility in him, not physical, but lodged in sudden, cloudy preoccupations. But he follows me with almost tender concern. When the track widens he comes alongside and proffers his water bottle by way of breaking silence. His Tamang people left Tibet more than a thousand years ago to settle in the mountains west of Everest, then scattered all through Nepal, and as we talk, I realise that he is not a highlander at all. His village is in the hills near Kathmandu, where his father, a cook, moved when the boy was three.

'The tradition in our village is like with Sherpa people. We came as horse soldiers, I don't know when, long ago. Now we go into trekking. Guides and porters. That's what we are, Tamangs.'

'But now you live in Kathmandu!' I warm to him, but my voice sounds edgy. Kathmandu is sunk in a turmoil of mass rural immigration, broken infrastructure, political corruption.

'Yes. We had to go. We Tamangs look for jobs. For education. But my family have a cottage in the village still. It is very quiet, very beautiful. My mother goes there to rent our land to other farmers. It's corn land, but it's too small.'

This was the plight of all Asia: the flight from the land. He loved and despised his village. There was no future there. He says: 'Everyone leaves for somewhere else. Not just for Kathmandu but India, the Gulf, even farther.'

Yet he half belongs to the village still. Like the cook and the horseman, he can shoulder the load of a mule. But he is touched by an urban gloss. His hair starts far back on a high forehead, tied in a ponytail, and his face has the lemony blandness of a sumo wrestler's, faintly androgynous.

He says: 'The village is full of old people now.'

On a path below us a woman is striding fast above the river. On her back a sick baby is bundled like a sad, balding toy. Iswor calls out to her. She is walking to Simikot to find medicine, she cries. She is quickly gone.

He stops for a moment. 'This is not like England.'

Here fifty babies die to every thousand born. I ask: 'You have children?'

He seems to wince. 'I'm not married. I'll wait ten years

before I marry. Yes, there are girls I like, but I'll wait. In the village, men marry at eighteen or twenty. But I've left that life behind.' Then, as if licensed at last to voice a pent-up question, he asks: 'And you? Why are you doing this, travelling alone?'

I cannot answer.

I am doing this on account of the dead.

Sometimes journeys begin long before their first step is taken. Mine, without my knowing, starts not long ago, in a hospital ward, as the last of my family dies. There is nothing strange in this, the state of being alone. The death of parents may bring resigned sadness, even a guilty freedom. Instead I need to leave a sign of their passage. My mother died just now, it seems, not in the way she wished; my father before her; my sister before that, at the age of twenty-one.

Time is unsteady here. Sometimes I am a boy again, trying to grasp the words *Never, never again*. Humans, it is said, cannot comprehend eternity, in time or space. We are better equipped to register the distance spanned by a village drumbeat. The sheerness of *never* is beyond us.

The sherpa's eyes stay mute on me, puzzled. Solitude here is an unsought peril. I joke: 'Nobody's fool enough to travel with me!'

It is already evening. Our feet grate over the stones. You cannot walk out your grief, I know, or absolve yourself of your survival, or bring anyone back. You are left with the desire only that things not be as they are. So you choose somewhere meaningful on the earth's surface, as if planning a secular pilgrimage. Yet the meaning is not your own. Then you go on a journey (it's my profession, after all), walking to a place beyond your own history, to the sound of the river flowing the other way. In the end you come to rest at a mountain that is holy to others.

The reason for this is beyond articulation. A journey is not a cure. It brings an illusion, only, of change, and becomes at best a spartan comfort.

Iswor looks robust, but he stops to complain quaintly of a mosquito bite on his hand, splaying his fingers for my inspection. They are chubby as a baby's, I tell him. We laugh and go on.

To ask of a journey *Why?* is to hear only my own silence. It is the wrong question (although there seems no other). Am I harrowing myself because the world is mortal? Whose pain am I purging? Not theirs. An old Tibetan monk tells me the soul has no memory. The dead do not feel their past.

Meanwhile the sun is setting with a perverse radiance behind us.

In the village of Tuling, at dusk, a family takes us in. Among the huddled houses, mud-roofed and half-plastered, theirs is one of the poorest, reached by a notched log ladder against the hillside. They live – a family of nine – in three narrow rooms. The walls are stucco and loose stones, built thick against the winter, pierced by a single window: a deep rectangle, closed by cracked cellophane. They have no furniture, no water. Their lavatory is a patch of ground scattered with rags.

Awkwardly we hunker on the mud floor: Iswor, the cook and I, feeling suddenly outsize. Our travelling kit – more than everything the family owns – is stacked against one wall. Everything we have looks excessive. Their possessions hang in a few bags from the beam ends poking through the plaster. A glaze of black flies shifts over the ceilings.

Lauri, the householder, sits with us, fervid and garrulous. He has moist, coal-black eyes. His ancient father and mother, his wife and five children come and go, or crouch round a rusty stove whose flue pokes through the ceiling. They are dressed almost in rags, ingrained with dirt, gaping at the elbow, shoulder, knee. The women walk on blackened feet – the children too, their skin striped harsh where sandals have once been. Three of the girls are pretty, but already knots of worry are puckering between their eyes.

At the other end of life, the two old people move oblivious among us: she like a tempest, he a wraith. She is hard-bodied, stick-thin. In the pitch-dark room beside us she is churning butter in a wooden trough, and barks to herself in angry phrases that Iswor doesn't translate. From time to time she emerges and lurches for the door beyond us, blind to our stares. Her head is twisted piratically in rags, but her ear lobes and nostrils are loaded with gold rings and pendants, still flaunting bridal wealth, and her ankles are bangled in brass.

Her husband sits outside in the last of the twilight. He has misted, dreaming eyes. He is dressed in what had once been white, with old-fashioned leggings and a long, tattered smock whose back is labelled enigmatically 'Cut Short'. He never speaks. His sacerdotal dress makes me wonder if he is not a leftover shaman – they survive alongside Buddhism in these hills. Only when the neighbours' children crowd to the door to gaze at the foreigner does he get to his feet and shoos them away with a tiny stick.

The family is so poor that at night they can offer us only a little of the heavy local rice. We mix it with our own lentils and spinach, and offer biscuits, and so combine our hospitalities, while Lauri's wife presides with her ladle and tureen, and the children cluster behind her, and Iswor translates our soft, fragmentary exchanges.

Lauri is alert and rueful: the brutal facts of his region's isolation have long ago dawned on him. 'The trouble is we have no education,' he says. 'Only that would save us. It's too late for my father and mother – you see them – and it's too late for me. I'm thirty-five. My wife too, she is quite uneducated.' She smiles faintly. 'But my children go to school now. We have hope for them, and for the boy. But five children is too many. We had them again and again.' He rolls his arms, laughing. 'But now at last we have a son! With us the girls marry and go away, but the sons stay. The son sees you through old age.' In the nearby villages, he says, the birth of a boy is greeted by a fusillade of buckshot; the birth of a girl, by silence.

In the dimness shed by a single bulb, fed by the village solar heater, his children sit cross-legged against the wall behind him, and stare out with the importunate sweetness of children in famine posters. The oldest girl, who was perhaps welcomed, wears a once-beautiful apple-green dress, embroidered with pink leaves and flowers; but the others descend in deepening rags and disappointment, until the miraculous fourth child – the boy – then plummet again to a tiny, simian girl with streaming nose, wearing the last cast-offs.

'Will the girls' marriages be arranged?' I ask. 'What if they fall in love?' Already the eldest showed a wilful spark.

Lauri says: 'That will be all right. That should be the way now, the new way. We won't mind what caste they choose either.'

'It'll be expensive.'

'Yes, of course, the bride should be given away with money. But if the family's too poor . . . then nothing.' He looks at the ground.

Caste was outlawed in Nepal forty years ago, Iswor whispers. But of course it continues in everyone's minds. These people are Thakuri, I know, proudly linked to a medieval dynasty of Nepalese kings. A shockingly simplified sketch of Nepal's ethnic jigsaw might divide the country into two peoples: the Nepalese lowlanders of Indian intrusion, and the resistant, Tibetan-related highlanders, to whom we are ascending. But whatever once coupled the Thakuri with wealth, it has long gone.

Winter is the worst time, Lauri says. For days the snows coop the villagers in their fort-like houses, while they burn firewood and wait. His rice field was not enough to sustain his family, so they have built a shack by the track above the village, hoping to sell things. It stocks some toothbrushes and a shelf of canned drinks. And they have a cow.

I fear for them. Their girls, in this world of village exogamy, may marry far away, and their son looks sickly. Yet not all the region is so poor. 'There are men who have two wives here, even more,' Lauri says. 'Their first marriage was probably arranged, the second made for love. So they keep two houses, one for each. My brother is one of them. He's happy.'

Tentatively, imagining a new cause of his poverty, I ask: 'And you? You have other wives?'

'No. I will only have this one.'

I ask softly: 'It was a love match?'

She touches his arm. They sometimes smile at one another.

'No, it was arranged.'

She is oddly beautiful. Poor food has left her slender after five children, and although her cheeks and forehead show the dents and scars of accidents, her features are delicate and regular. Only when her mother-in-law passes near her do I see with a shock what she may become. Eerily they share the same facial structure, but the old woman's skin is ploughed by vertical ridges, and her mouth hangs slack. Both women show dainty, level teeth, and the older's golden jewellery is echoed glittering round the younger's throat and face. But all the frailer ornaments the daughter-in-law wears – her eggshell-blue choker and coils of crimson beads, the coral necklace gleaming in the cleft of her torn dress – have long ago dropped from the older woman, if she ever owned them.

Now her daughter-in-law is gaily ladling out fresh rice, her laughter like a squirrel's chattering, while the oldest girl – with the same haunting, regular face – peers over her shoulder, and the old woman mutters alongside with an anger so fierce and private that it becomes intrusive to look at her.

Later I go out into the clear night. It is still warm. The monsoons are late this year, and have not yet hit the Kathmandu valley, let alone up here. On the fringe of Lauri's ground, by a brushwood corral where the cow sleeps close to the cliff edge, stands a white-plastered turret, perforated by little holes for offerings, and stuck with a rusty trident: the family shrine. Its only gifts are chunks of local marble laid outside its niches. In the starlight it looks like a pallid dovecote.

Who is worshipped here? I wonder. But when I ask Lauri, he sinks into a vague, confusing answer. The Hindu pantheon of his people mingles with other, more shadowy powers. He speaks uneasily of Masto, an ancient shamanic god, or family of gods. Masto cannot precisely be identified. No images depict him, but sometimes, through a medium, he dances and speaks.

'Three times a year our family gathers for a ceremony at the altar,' Lauri says. 'At time of the full moon. Then my father leads us in worship . . .'

His father sits under the stars long after we have turned in, while his mother lies with the children in a room beside us, and he and his wife sleep in the storeroom beyond. A dirty cloth has been laid on the floor, where we lie in a row, Iswor complaining. Nestling in the ceiling among beams and broken slats, cicadas send up a high, seamless cheeping, which must have been sounding unnoticed all evening. I lie listening to the rustle of sparrows under the eaves, the howl of dogs. In the room nearby a child sobs, and the retching and spitting of the old woman goes on for hours. Two or three times she bursts in and charges like a hurricane across the room, her hair loosed in an astonishing black flood, and the outer door flies open on a gash of stars as she rushes a naked child into the lavatory patch. They return in silence,

15

and peace descends for an hour or two. The cicadas have gone dumb, and the noises of restless breathing have stilled.

Then, like another breathing going on unheard, the sigh of the great river rises from below.

CHAPTER TWO

· · · · · · ·

I wake up to a stormy sky and a sallow light streaking the mountains to the east. Lauri's children gather round to gaze as we pack our magic things: a compass, a diode flashlight, some miniature binoculars. We eat a breakfast of boiled rice on the rooftop, while the village stirs beneath us. In the rocks near the river a mob of vultures is hopping and floundering around a dead buffalo. Then we hit trouble. Our horse drover cannot go on: his mare is lame, he says. In the warmth of the previous evening, a villager had offered to join us with his own horse, but now he is afraid. He has a weak heart, he says; we are ascending too high.

So Iswor and Ram shoulder a double load – they must be carrying over a hundred pounds each – and hope to find a baggage animal somewhere ahead. All morning the path is easy. Behind us Tuling drops out of sight, but for another mile its paddy fields shine emerald above the river, and higher up ripple yellow terraces where barley and buckwheat are ready for cutting. Then the way narrows and the great trees – spruce, maple, cypress – throng darkly to the river. Ahead the mountains are tremulous with cloud. It rolls from their clefts and seethes round their summits like battle smoke. But we are walking in sunshine, still barely making height. Shrubs of papery cistus bank along our path, with many low, creeping rock plants, and flocks of butter-flies blow like confetti over the stones.

Gradually we are swinging north-west towards the Nala Kankar Himal, which rises three and a half miles above sea level as it shelves into Tibet. By noon the May sun is burning. Iswor carries his monstrous load without concern, rigged out in summer shorts and a headstrap. His heavy calves taper to sturdy ankles in slack, oversize boots. Some-times, when avalanches sever the track, he puzzles that these were not there before. In the past few years, with failing rains, the soil has eroded deeper, and we find ourselves clattering across stilled torrents of multicoloured rocks – veined marble, blood-red, crystalline grey – torn from the hillsides. But high above the far bank, steeper than ours, waterfalls come floating down in 300-foot drops, then vanish into wooded gullies and re-emerge to fall again in ropes of glittering light.

The Karnali itself – we are descending imperceptibly to it – is no longer an immured thread. It is pristine and violent. Its waters seethe and plunge among half-submerged boulders, alternately baulked and released, flooding into furious eddies and slipstreams – a beautiful grey-green commotion in momentary drift, then battered to white foam again. In local lore the rocks that strew it are silver fish from the Ganges that could struggle no further upriver. Here the Karnali seems less sacred than primitive and untouched. Yet it finds its source near the lakes beside holy Kailas, and sanctity will descend on it downriver, of course, with silt and pollution, as it eases into the Ganges plain.

We walk under apricot and walnut trees through the last silent Thakuri villages, past thinning paddy fields. Among the traders along the track, the Thakuri are giving way to stocky Bhotia people. Under their bobble hats the faces are broader, more Mongoloid: hardy men with polished cheekbones who carry their goods on their backs in wooden frames and lead horses slung with brushwood and fodder. Some, from the Tibetan borderlands, are driving buffalo and mule trains laden with Chinese clothes and cigarettes.

For centuries Nepal was Tibet's chief link with the outside world, and their trade goes back to prehistory. Here, in the country's west, Tibetans bartered their salt and wool for lowland grains, as they still do, and even in the early twentieth century, after many trade routes were diverted to British India, this Himalayan porterage survived.

Now, within a few hours, we have passed the outer reach of Indian influence and crossed into another world. In origin the local Bhotias are Tibetan Buddhists, and we are entering a sanctity more remote and arcane than the Hindu. The cairns of piled stones that mark the high passes are spiked with poles where prayer flags fly. Who hung them in these lonely defiles we cannot tell. As the wind funnels through the passes, their inscriptions stream in faded tatters. With every flutter, it is believed, the wind disperses their prayer into the world, to ease the suffering of all sentient beings. And they will propitiate whatever capricious mountain gods control the pass.

I touch them gingerly: the Tibetan script that I do not understand. I have seen them before in China and in regions of Tibetan exile, and every time they stir a poignant wonder.

19

They glare in five primary colours, embodying earth, air, fire, water and sky. Like the prayer wheels that circle holy sites or turn in the hands of pilgrims, they redeem the world by the mystique of words. Some, near monasteries, are even turned by flowing water. Many are stamped with the wind horse, who flies their mantras on his jewelled back; others with the saint Padmasambhava, who restored Buddhism to Tibet. Iswor circles them reverently, clockwise. I follow him, glad, for some reason, of his faith. Sometimes the flags are so thinned that their prayers are as diaphanous as cobwebs. But this, Iswor says, does not matter. The air is already printed with their words.

Gently it starts to rain. At first we ignore this, but underfoot the path grows treacherous, sometimes winding 300 feet vertically above the river – and for the first time Iswor stops not for me, but to rest his burdened back against the rock. Then we change into waterproofs, and go on. Now water surrounds us. It churns through the ravine below, gushes out of every rock face, sheets down from the sky. I raise my face to it, hoping that it augurs the monsoons at last. Two and three hundred feet above us waterfalls loose themselves from the cliffs and spill down past giant ferns and bamboos almost to our feet. Here, where the Karnali squeezes between sheer walls, a narrow path has been hacked from the cliff side. We peer dizzyingly down to glimpse the river boiling through a canyon hung with vertical crevices, black and yellow. Beyond, the land grows ever more savage and precipitous. Our stone-littered track goes switchbacking emptily for miles. Intermittently, when the rain clears, we see the 23,000-foot snows of Saipal Himal to our south. The only person we pass is a cheery Bhotia woman smoking through a clay tube and cradling a potful of cannabis.

An hour later, in weak sunlight, we stop by a rocky over-hang. Evening is coming on. We munch on cheese and biscuits, and Iswor dozes. Idly I spread a map on the ground, trying to locate our position on a grander scale: Dehra Dun . . . Lucknow . . . Ladakh in the north . . . Lhasa . . . Delhi . . . Then, with a shock, just beyond the border in India, I glimpse the name. Naini Tal! It strikes me with a strange, sad excitement. I'd sometimes wondered where it was. Eighty years ago my father had served in India as a soldier, and Naini Tal sounded through my childhood with a boundless romance. Incredulously I measure the distance again. On the map it is only a hand's breadth away from where I sit (or 140 miles, as the crow flies). Naini Tal, Bhim Tal, Chanda: they were engraved on shields beneath the mounted heads of leopards and deer in my parents' dining room. Naini Tal was the hill station from which my father had hunted big game.

I lie on the rocks, dreaming into another age. I found his hunting records preserved among early photograph albums after my mother's death. The episodes these albums em-balm are, I suppose, the expected ones of their place and time: the callow young officers in pith helmets and knee-length shorts, marching in the scrublands of the Central Provinces or jokingly astride their Enfield motorbikes; the army wives and daughters in perms and cloche hats; scenes of pig-sticking and the Madras Hunt.

But my father's *shikar* records were different. In these he became solitary, perhaps himself. As early as 1925, at the age of twenty-one, he was departing alone into the jungle. The accounts of his hunting are as detailed and exact as if he were on campaign, penned in white ink on the black pages of photo albums. The hand-drawn maps – pin-pointing areas of tiger, blackbuck or mouse deer – are meticulous, even beautiful, and his observations sometimes have the near-scientific exactitude of a Victorian explorer's. The qualities that made him a wartime soldier, I realise, were first put into practice here.

Leafing through these records, I sense too the strangely intimate bond of hunter with prey, especially with the big cats – 'old man stripes' he calls the tiger that eludes him, 'old man spots' the leopards he kills. Mixed with the sportsman's chivalric code – the strictly selected victims, the shame and distress at wounding – I hear the fascinated voice of the naturalist he had youthfully wanted to be. He applied an almost loving attention to the animals he was slaying: their gait, their sounds. The sharp *pook* of the sambhu and the deep, eerie *owoon* of the tiger make a noise in these pages not only for their significance to the hunter but as phenomena in themselves.

My father grew up in another age. Game was fairly plentiful in India then, and its killing accepted. The deer and pig he shot were eaten round the campfire, and leopards threatened local livestock and even children. Yet sometimes I struggle to understand. I gaze at the young man, my father, posed unsmiling above his kill. A great black bear is sprawled like a soft toy before him, its legs stiff in death; he squats above a seven-foot leopard carcass, or sits on the haunch of a dead bison, his Winchester against his knees. But the photographs are no more than blown-up snapshots, taken by his tracker, and his face looks less resolved than I ever remember it, and I do not know him.

Was it easier, in those times, to kill? Once, while he was hunting leopard, he wrote, 'A fine male bear came through the jungle from behind, and stood on a rock, all four feet together, sniffing the air very suspiciously. He appeared pretty silently without any previous warning, as is usually the case. Finally he came forward a little way, darted back, and then walked off at an angle from my tree. This necessitated a hurried shot in the kidneys, when the poor creature started whimpering like a human child. Two more hurried shots put him out of his misery.'

As a boy I liked to lie on this bear – it had been turned into a rug by then, complete with stuffed head – and to rest my face on its own.

For my father, the terrain around Naini Tal rose steeply eastward around minor Ganges tributaries before reaching the Karnali, where I now lie in the sun. He described it as 'rolling tree jungle', reaching to thick pine forest, and it was here that he shot the huge leopard that snarled for sixty years on my parents' dining room wall. He was only sad, he wrote, that my mother did not witness the kill – he had been married three years by then. The month before, with my mother Evelyn crouched in the dark beside him, he had shot a leopard near Hyderabad. He wrote simply: 'Took neck shot. Although many dead leaves, no sound. Eve very thrilled.'

But she secretly recoiled. Animals were always close to

her. Even on her wedding day she had led a pet Dalmatian on a silk leash. In India she thrilled to the adventure, but hated the killing. Sometimes, torn by disloyalty, she hoped his bullet would miss. All this he never knew. Back in England, the low Tudor walls of our house sprouted a stuffed wildlife that made me dizzy with excitement as a boy. Five leopards and two bears gaped from the walls or spread over the floor. A chital master stag with three-foot antlers hung above one stairway; a wolf grinned in the back lavatory; from upstairs passages the gentle eyes of chausingha and chinkara gazelles enchanted my sister Carol. Hugest of all, the taxidermised head of a bison overhung one fireplace. My father had felled it at some risk, with a single hard-nose cartridge to the brain. 'A fine old bull, 17 years old,' he recorded, 'though the horns unfortunately were much worn. No grazing teeth at all. Covered him with brambles, and returned to camp singing sweetly.' In time the great beast threatened posthumously to tear down the fireplace wall, and was exiled to the garage. From there, years later, somebody stole him.

Yet my father, I suspect was not a born hunter. Once or twice in his journal he simply doesn't fire, just watches the animal move splendidly away, and cannot explain himself. In middle age, although living in the Sussex countryside, he gave up shooting altogether. He preferred to walk in the woodlands and observe the calls and flight of birds. He would return glowing to report a cock pheasant glittering by a sunset field, or the zigzag trajectory of a snipe. The Indian trophies remained on the walls, although my mother never cared for them. But she knew better than I what they meant to him, and she never hinted her misgiving, so that in my adult eyes they became her secret gift to him.

My father neither boasted nor apologised for them. Compared to the monotonous inevitability of the abattoir, he might have said, the sporting rifle was a fine thing. In his journals he wrote that the jungle taught him three lessons: patience, endurance, and the ability to survive disappointment. In time he would need them all.

The Indian foothills steepen near the Nepalese border, and the people change. The mustachioed, mahogany faces of trackers and beaters that stare from my father's snapshots are replaced by paler, trimmer men. Towards sunset, as Iswor and I approach the village of Kermi, we are overtaken by youths indistinguishable from Tibetans, by broad-faced women with centrally parted hair and shining pigtails. I had expected the Bhotia inhabitants, low caste and isolated, to be poorer than the Thakuri, but instead the village looks happier, its stone houses built firm against the hillside, Maoist slogans dimming on their walls, and the men who greet us are alert and soft-spoken. The Thakuri downriver, it seems, pride themselves on caste, but it is the despised and stranded Bhotia who are forced into greater trading enterprise. Or so Iswor tells me.

Close by the village, to my astonishment, we cross a stream whose waters flow warm against our hands, and bluish smoke drifts in the gully above. Curious, we follow the path up, and soon the stink of sulphur rises above green-tinted rocks. A young woman is bathing in the strange river, naked to the waist, and turns from us unperturbed. We reach a clearing where the stream is boiling hot to the touch. The frames of rotten beds stretch over it, and the banks are scattered with palliasses of disintegrated brushwood, burnt yellow by the fumes. In January, a farmer tells us, villagers come out and sleep for nights on end above the vaporous river – it boosts their health in winter, they say – then bathe each morning in the freezing springs nearby.

We camp a mile beyond, where Ram, the cook, who has long preceded us, pitches my tent. This regimen will be repeated many nights. Ram, who has the lungs of a mountaineer, disappears every morning over the track ahead of us, until we discover him at evening on level camping ground, with our tents pitched and a crude supper on the boil. Tonight too he has found a Thakuri horse drover who will accompany us to the frontier: a shaggy, silent man named Dhabu, who rarely takes his eyes from me. We eat all together in a half-built stone hut where they lay out their sleeping bags among a litter of aluminium pots and pans. Iswor lights candles in the crevices of the walls, while Ram serves up noodles and tinned tuna from an ancient gas stove labelled 'Quality 3'.

At sunset the temperature plummets and a wind blows through the empty window frames and snuffs the candles one by one. But we are in high spirits, everyone glad of Dhabu's grey stallion cropping the weeds outside. Like my father, I am happy in these solitudes, sleeping in the pure air above the great river. Iswor and Ram, fellow Tamangs, talk non-stop in the soft Nepali that I strain hopelessly to understand, while Dhabu crouches in the darkest corner, tongue-tied, watching me. As the candles gutter, their faces darken and simplify. I rouse myself at last and go out to my tent, where I empty my backpack and try to write by torch-light. Instead, withdrawn into my sleeping bag, oblivious of the rock under my spine, I drop into sleep.

Hours later, I am woken by a snuffling and nudging at the canvas against my head. Crawling from my sleeping bag, too tired to be alarmed, I open my tent flap on a huge, stooping head with red-tasselled ears. Somebody's yak has wandered down from Kermi in the starlight, lost.

CHAPTER THREE
· · · · · · ·

Overnight the rain has cleaned the earth, blowing lightly up the valley from the east, then receding at dawn. From the track below rise the shouts and whistles of traders, driving their packhorses towards Simikot. I emerge from my tent to a sky washed clear. The wind has gone. Birds are singing in the shrubs. Ahead the river winds between mountain spurs that recede and overlap ever fainter, before misting away through gullies dense with deciduous forest. The water sounds below like smothered talking. Files of solitary pines patrol the hilltops above. And the last horizon to which the river points – far away under high cirrus cloud – seals the sky in a glistening, snow-lit wall to which we are unimaginably going.

Ram and Iswor crouch alternately at my tent flap at sunrise, bringing lukewarm coffee, a bowl of shaving water, a breakfast of chapati and jam. They treat me with dutiful reserve. They wash in a freezing rivulet. Within half an hour the horse is laden with rope-lashed tents and ground-sheets and blackened kitchen ware, and we are moving into the dawn.

This is the hour of elation. You fancy you are walking into a pristine land. There is no sign, for a while, that it has ever been peopled. Your steps fall light. The trees chatter with birdsong and the river, invisible below, roars in its green chasms. It will be an hour, perhaps, before your body or mind habituates. You go as if dreaming. Rock pigeons are flitting between cliff crevices below, and the sun climbs warm behind you.

The terrain looks thin-covered, yet wherever the valley sides ease out of sheer rock, tremendous trees take hold. Firs and hundred-foot blue pines bank up with cypress and poplar in precipitous tiers, and weeping spruces thrust along the middle slopes. Soon we are among them, ascending in their shadow. As we toil up close to 10,000 feet, the heights that circle round us darken, crows croak from the pine tops and we are tramping among powder-grey boulders. A smiling woman passes by us, led by a youth. She is lovely, and mad, her ears hung with gold. They are gone before we can speak with them. The pines look diseased around us. They die upright, leafless and charred-looking, their stripped branches all intact, like ruined totem poles. A small village is here, whose terraces of buckwheat and potatoes shelve down to the river. Its people fell the pines for trade, and fill me with misgiving for these near-untouched forests.

We are entering the mountains as if following a jagged knife thrust. The smallest earth tremor, I feel, will snuff us out. Rather than making height, we are going deep. Whenever the valley walls part, the pinnacles of ice-bound mountains gleam beyond, and razor-sharp palisades, scarred with snow melt, stream up into powder-puff clouds. Such views grow hypnotic, especially, in the valley cleft ahead. I wait for any change in its parapets, any sign of a breach into

Tibet. But they shift with the twisting river like stage scenery, as if conspiring in the old mystique of Tibet as an inaccessible otherworld.

I am travelling with this mystique myself, I know. It has grown out of childhood, and adolescent reading. This looking-glass Tibet is a realm of ancient learning lost to the rest of the world, ruled by a lineage of monks who are reincarnations of divinity. Recessed beyond the greatest mountain barrier on earth, in plateaux of cold purity, it floats in its own time. It is a land forbidden to intruders not by human agency but by some mystical interdiction. So it resonates like the memory of something lost, a survival from a purer time, less a country than a region in the mind. Perhaps it holds the keys to the afterlife.

The source of these imaginings is a complex one. The tiny handful of early European travellers to Tibet brought back contradictory records, portraying a land of faith and squalor, ruled by a lama elite at once oppressive and benign. Morality coexisted confusingly with idleness and rank superstition. As Tibet's Buddhist isolation deepened into the nineteenth century, infected by Chinese xenophobia and an isolationist Nepal, Europeans could enter it only by subterfuge, often in disguise. The few who did so created a country – refracted through Victorian eyes – peopled by pious primitives steeped in magic and sexual depravity (polyandry was rife) and so perverse that the only wheels they permitted were those for generating prayer.

Then, towards the end of the century, just as European scholarship began to grapple with a more porous Tibet, a cloud of spiritual expectancy brewed up. It took bizarre forms. The notorious Madame Blavatsky, founder of the Theosophical Society, claimed guidance from a lost Atlantean kingdom in Tibet – a brotherhood later exposed as non-existent. Soon Tibet was rumoured a laboratory of occult miracles, where the paranormal was studied as a science. Its monks performed prodigies of telepathy and sonic power, moving rocks by their voices alone. Its yogis levitated and flew. Its statues spoke. The *lung-pa*, 'wind men', after extremes of meditation, could speed like ghosts across the landscape, barely touching the ground. And all through the land were hidden sacred and prophetic texts, buried by great masters centuries before, to be unearthed only when the time was ripe. The country's mystique touched even Rudyard Kipling's *Kim*; and when Conan Doyle was forced by public demand to resurrect Sherlock Holmes from the dead, he opted for Tibet as the country in which Holmes might temporarily but convincingly have disappeared.

The fantasy of Tibet as an exalted sanctuary continued far into the twentieth century, and has never quite stilled. The country's religion, which Victorians had considered a distant and decadent deviation from the Buddha's truth, was gradually hailed, on the contrary, as the refined pinnacle of a developed faith, and its scriptures as a treasure house embalmed by Tibet's isolation. The sense of a miraculously preserved past was crucial to the myth. The country had a dreamlike quality, as if time had stopped. Travellers might feel themselves re-entering childhood, or an innocent and unruly unconscious. Others likened the voyage through Tibet, for all its mountain fastness, to a descent into the underworld, and the burgeoning popularity of *The Tibetan*

Book of the Dead, variously translated, shed its strangeness even on my own journey.

As the West reeled in disillusion through two world wars, the last strictures on Tibet faded away. It became a site of pure human longing. The name Shangri-La had entered the language through the mythic Tibetan utopia of James Hilton's novel *Lost Horizon*, published in 1933, whose seers would redeem the world after its self-destruction. And something of this millennial yearning went on clinging to the country, shadowed by a foreboding at its fragility once it was exposed to the outer world.

These fantasies, of course, were distorted echoes of the earthly Tibet. The country was born in violence – most of its early kings died young – and for centuries it waged aggressive war against itself and others. In this bitter land and climate the people were prey to disease and earthquake, and within living memory worked as indentured labour for an often callous monkhood. The pious Buddhist folk whom travellers knew as gentle, cheerful and honest were haunted by evil spirits and by starvation. Even pilgrims to Kailas were sometimes so impoverished that they took to banditry, which might be punished by public mutilation.

Only after the Chinese invasion of Tibet in 1959 did the fantasy finally fragment. After the Dalai Lama, with much of the monastic elite, fled into India and beyond, Tibet itself – while never quite emptied of sanctity in the Western mind – became a place of violated innocence, at first brutally persecuted by the Chinese, then half sanitised for the secular gaze. As its homeless Buddhism opened to the West – whether as a faith, a therapy or a fashionable cult – the country itself was lost. In exile, Tibetans looked back (if they remembered) on a land of pained wish-fulfilment.

The country softens and purifies in their absence. The meadows grow apple green, the women beautiful. This is the land of yearning.

Three weeks ago it covered the walls of my hotel in Kathmandu with frescoes of pure consolation: a dream world of herdsmen in trimmed furs and synthetic colours.

The hotel's owner was a refugee made good. A portrait of the Dalai Lama hung over the reception desk, and photographs of Lhasa in 1937 lined the passages. I asked the receptionist – his hair was flecked with grey – if he could ever go back. Back? he said. He had never been. His parents fled in 1959, and he was born in exile. 'If I tried to get in, there would be trouble. It's all right for you. It's not your country. But the border guards can tell us by our faces.'

I roamed the rooms unhappily, where the pillars dripped with painted gold and the murals were fairy-tale. They did not even depict a remembered country – the land that changes in the exiles' absence until they are unfit to return. It was a land that never existed at all. Its painted sheep grazed in eternal summer. Nomad tea-drinkers picnicked beside their tents, while an old man sang to his long-stemmed lute, and young men listened. Behind them the cloud-enfolded monasteries dreamed on far hills. And beyond these the perfect hemisphere of Mount Kailas shone like an egg in its cup of mountains, where cave-dwelling hermits radiated the light of other-knowledge, and sanctified the land with prayer.

I wondered again where I was going. This painted mountain had been abstracted into paradise, and turned inert. But to believers, the earthly Kailas is a ladder between light and darkness – its foundations are in hell – and a site of redemptive power. It stirs in the real world, for which the Chinese must fear it. It is older than they.

We come to a high pass. Iswor has preceded me and is resting against a tree, his backpack dropped. We are halfway between Kermi and Yangar villages, and the sun is still high. A few yards shy of the crest, before the valley drops from sight behind us, stretches a short wall of loose stones.

'Go round it!' Iswor is rotating his arm clockwise.

I had imagined it a bank of scree cleared from the track. But now I am peering at rocks and stones stacked carefully together. Some are pearl-grey granite, others pitted marble, others the colour of honey or rust. However hard their surfaces, they are all carved with prayers. Several hundred there must be, faded, like a lost language. Their mantras flow with a level delicacy, and sometimes follow the curves and veins of the stone. Many rocks – the most beautiful – are not incised at all. Instead they are chiselled away so that the words stand out in relief, as if freed from the heart of the rock, and the stone itself were speaking. Iswor stares at them, but cannot translate. 'This is monks' language,' he says.

I recognise the downstrokes of the Buddhist refrain, *Om mani padme hum,* which murmurs all day in the mouths of the devout. This invocation to the goddess of compassion – 'O you who hold the jewelled [rosary] and the lotus!' – has drowned in centuries of esoteric interpretation. Other stones show longer mantras, all in Tibetan script. Whole books, perhaps, are scattered in these rocks. Another carving contains the Buddha's teaching on the illusoriness of things. So this too is set in stone: that all is transitory.

To circle these walls, as we do, is said to activate all the prayers in them again. They are quaintly moving in their solitude. They must have been built up over generations: stones carved for traders, pilgrims, monks, placed here to appease the spirits of the place – passes are always dangerous – and to breathe compassion to the outer world.

As we descend into the valley beyond, Iswor says the wall is murmuring behind us.

We go down among towering trees to where the Salle Khola tributary joins the Karnali among groves of wild marijuana. Dropping through these cathedral shadows with the first breath of evening, we are intruding on a zone of windless silence. Our boots dislodge cascades of shale or rustle over beds of pine needles. Giant firs and pines surge up between prickly oak and hemlock, and spruce trees hang their pink cones a hundred feet above. Iswor is singing Kathmandu pop songs to himself, but he is far behind me, so that the sudden, solitary drilling of a woodpecker echoes sharp, like a memory, in the valley. I stop in surprise. I try to glimpse the bird, but cannot. The familiar sound intrudes like an eerie signal, as if I were being benignly followed. The woodpecker goes silent; then after a minute, like an echo from childhood, sounds the call of a cuckoo. I have read about Himalayan birds before leaving, but cannot tell if this is the

common or the Oriental cuckoo. For the cuckoo is comi-
cally complicated. Thus: 'The Oriental Cuckoo (*Cuculus
optatus*) is a bird belonging to the genus Cuculus in the
cuckoo family Cuculidae . . . Some authors use the names
Horsfield's Cuckoo for *optatus* and Oriental Cuckoo for
saturatus while others use Oriental Cuckoo for *optatus* and
Himalayan Cuckoo for *saturatus* . . .' But both, it seems, sound
like a cuckoo clock, and I stop long minutes under the great
trees, listening, absurdly entranced, to *optatus* or *saturatus*.

There are familiar shrubs too. Jasmine, syringa and a
teeming species of viburnum have fringed our track for
two days, and now spread their foliage in the clearings.
Sometimes I have the illusion of walking through a ruined
English garden. Generations of botanists, after all, brought
back the Himalaya to Europe, tenderly crated, and their
specimens are all about us. Sunlight opens the papery white
flowers of rock roses and potentilla over the hillsides. I
locate honeysuckle, mimosa, dogwood; and tortoiseshell
butterflies are floating among faded buddleia.

A wonky tin bridge spans the Salle Khola. The stream
flows jade green like the Karnali, whose noise is hollow and
far away now, bellowing in constricted chasms. Here, for a
few hundred yards, the mountains' upheaval levels out.
Some goatherds are corralling their flocks among boulders,
and a solitary farmer passes us, cradling two chickens. On
the far bank the trees crowd in again – deciduous and ever-
green together – and nothing exists but tumbling water and
this dense, seamless foliage. Once a voice screams a warning
above us and we hear the rumbling start of rocks moving.
Two rams are butting along the scarp vertically above, while

their goatherd panics. Iswor and I freeze on the path. The rocks come crashing down between us in twos and threes, bounce on the track then spin on like giant flints to the river, while above us the wild goat girl scrambles upwards cursing her charges and hurling stones.

Two hours later, in the waning light, we are ambling alongside the Karnali through broad, smooth grasslands. The river runs strong and undepleted as we approach the village of Yalbang. Our path is littered with horse droppings and discarded harness. From somewhere the two-note song of *saturatus* (or *optatus*) follows us along the valley. Our horse drover, Dhabu, is waiting for us here, grazing his stallion Moti, Pearl, on the sudden grass. We sit on rocks to eat, while I wonder aloud if a family in Yalbang will take us in.

Iswor says grimly, in his troubled English: 'You will die here.'

A faint alarm. 'Die here? Who will kill me?'

He laughs curtly. 'Not "die here". I said "You will *diarrhoea*." These people dirty.'

Dhabu laughs too, from habit. His hazel eyes glitter in a swarthy face. Some unspoken divide exists between him and Iswor and Ram, not of caste (for he is Thakuri) but of education. Born in these wild valleys, he never went to school. Now he sits on a rock apart to stare at me, his eyes divided by a twitch of puzzlement. He always eats last and out of sight, and when I offer him anything – a slice of apple or a sweet – he accepts it with surprise and mute confusion, extending both hands to receive it.

Iswor, meanwhile, is rinsing his long hair in the river – he is girlishly proud of it. He comes to sit by me as I scroll back snapshots in my camera. On its monitor a slender woman appears in an Italian garden.

He asks: 'Who is that?'

'That is my partner.'

He stares at her. 'She is great beauty.'

She is smiling beneath the Tivoli waterfall. It had been hard to leave her. In Kathmandu her voice had reached me over the telephone from 8,000 miles away: 'Don't think of me.' The phone in the monastic guest house blurs her sound away. 'Think of where you are.'

So she gives her imprimatur to the traveller's cruelty: to the fading of his shared, past life before the rush of the new.

I ask Iswor: 'You have a girlfriend?'

'No, I don't want. In Nepal, if you sleep with one of these village girls' – he gestures at the forest – 'you have to marry her within a year. But I want an educated woman, and my life is too poor. How can I ask her to wait ten years? She wouldn't trust me. She'd say you'll go, you'll leave. And many people go from here – to the Gulf especially. But it's a bad life there. I tried that once. I planned to go and work as somebody's bodyguard. I even signed up. But my parents said no, no, you'll be killed. So I'm here, working as a guide. But there's no work now. Only you.'

He is smiling, perhaps secretly relieved at his parents' prohibition. He says: 'In the city, we are like you in the West now. Men can marry at thirty-five or later. I'll wait.'

But how can he wait so long, I wonder, without a woman?

'Oh that is all right,' he says. 'I understand about love . . . I know about it.' When he thrusts back the damp hair from his forehead, his bland features remind me disquietingly of Mao Zedong.

'Love?' I ask. 'How can you know?'

'I've read the magazines. I've seen the films. I'll have two children, a boy and a girl, and I'll make sure they're educated.' He glances at Dhabu, who is grinning to himself, uneducated, on a rock. 'I've read about it all.'

Ahead of us, from the ridges above Yalbang, a white pinnacle shoots into the sky. It is a Buddhist stupa – a hill-side memorial above a perched monastery – and it touches our last hour of walking with a premonition of Tibet. Then a man runs down at us from the cave where he is camped and lifts his hands quivering above his head. He is suffering from headache, begging for medicine. But Dhabu has gone ahead with our baggage, and I can give the man nothing. I curse myself as we leave him. I must remember to carry aspirin at least.

Soon afterwards the river bends under a high promontory, crowned by a rough-stoned tower, and the valley opens round the scattered homes of Yalbang. Two orange triangles fleck the rocks, where Ram has pitched our tents.

CHAPTER FOUR

· · · · · · ·

Black crows are picking over the campsite. The dawn sky is split violently in two. Rain clouds are pouring through the valleys beneath us, fading the foothills into one another and blurring the crests of Sisne Hind fifty miles beyond. But to the north-east the sky is blue over Tibet. Just above us the monastery is stirring into prayer, and beyond it a long, snow-glazed skyline has caught the first light.

The boulder-thickened hillside beside me is swarming with tiny children. The labyrinthine rocks echo with their laughter and screaming. A tribe of leprechauns might be running amok there. But they are dressed in pink jumpsuits stamped with Mickey Mouse or blazoned 'Going It' or 'The Vogue Current'. Under their bobble hats their cheeks are flushed crimson and their hair coerced into pigtails or page-boy crops. They seem insanely happy.

The school that has sprouted in this desolation, I discover, is so far from its pupils' homes that most remain here for nine months of the year, sleeping in bunk dormitories. Their headmaster is a gentle Bhotia, who shows me proudly round the mud-floored and stone-walled classrooms. Until three years ago the place was occupied by Maoists, who periodically fought the Nepalese army here while the children tried to go to school. Now the little assembly hall doubles as a Buddhist temple, on whose makeshift altar the teacher lifts a cloth from a picture of Padmasambhava, the great magician-saint revered of Tibet. We sit at last in a corner of the kitchen, resting under suspended ranks of bloodied yak sinews, while two Tibetan servant women brew up something on a stove at our feet.

I wonder how this middle-aged teacher, with his quiet, easy English, had ended up here, three days' walk from Simikot, the roadless village capital of the poorest district in the country. But he laughs this away. He was born here in Humla province, he says, and distances are not the same for him as for me. He has the deep lungs of his people; he can walk to Simikot in a single day; his wife takes two.

'I once worked in Kathmandu, in better times. I started a carpet factory using Tibetan wool and Tibetan weavers. That wool is beautiful, very strong, and Westerners loved it. But then the Maoists came. I had to increase wages. The cost of everything went up, and we collapsed. So I came here.'

The weaving of the small, high-coloured Tibetan rugs, I knew, had withered also under the impact of a different Western taste, then died with the global recession. Had he, I wondered, used child labour? He might have thought it kind. And in the last few years Maoist militias and corrupt police descended like vultures on the beleaguered factories.

'But it is not bad here,' he says. 'The children are poor, and need us.' Education obsesses these villages. Only one in five people is literate. 'In the winter snows we have to close, and everyone goes home.'

'Where is your home?'

'My family has scattered. My wife is sometimes here with me. But my son is a monk in India.' He adds with an odd, anxious pride: 'My daughter is a student.'

'Where is she?' I wonder if she attends the secondary school in Simikot, or is even in Kathmandu.

But he says: 'She's in Alabama, at college. She got a scholarship. She says it's a lovely place, but she can't find work to pay her tuition fees. And the exams are hard.'

So she is 9,000 miles away, and he cannot sustain her. He is afraid, I sense, that something will pull her away, and that he will lose her. So he talks on unhappily in this rough-walled dungeon, under the dripping yak sinews, while his daughter sits in her sorority in Alabama, fretting about her grades.

He says: 'She cannot afford to come home.'

A low wall surrounds the monastery. Under its gateway, topped by the Wheel of the Law, a woman is leading her little son round an enormous cylindrical prayer wheel. It creaks into motion only when he adds his tiny force to hers, and their laughter ripples out. Beyond the gate a big courtyard opens up, ringed by a two-storey arcade of derelict or half-built rooms. At its centre the temple comes as a vivid shock, huge and enigmatic in this solitude. Its bright-painted porch and double tier of casement windows, ochre and scarlet, and its roof of orange-coated iron seem daubed like make-up on a more ancient structure. But in fact the temple is barely twenty-five years old, raised in Tibetan exile.

I wander the arcades, past flaking plaster and smashed windows. A chill wind has got up. All around, the tree-hung mountains seem to be pouring against the walls. Across the courtyard a sagging cable, where crows perch, brings weak electricity from a village upriver. I press my nose to a grimed window and see a blanket and a coarse table and a child's face rising to meet mine through the glass, grinning: a boy novice surprised at study.

Meanwhile, from inside the temple throbs a deep, murmurous chant, as if a huge beehive were stirring. Through these thick walls it resounds like cosmic muttering, its rhythm quick but subdued. Some hundred monks are praying there. The temple seems built in sad memory of their homeland. The inward slope of its white-plastered walls, the bright eaves and window frames, the stucco medallions lifting off orange friezes, all echo the lost country to the north.

The abbot who emerges from the prayer hall carries more authority than his thirty years. When I wonder at such a monastery in this isolation – there are 150 monks and novices here – he answers with a strange sacred history. Over a century ago, he says, a revered teacher passed away near Mount Kailas – he 'took rainbow body', becoming pure light – leaving behind a disciple who built a famous monastery there. Such vanishments into astral bodies were more common in the old days, he says. Lamas and ascetics simply disappeared, leaving behind only their hair or fingernails. But in time the disciple died, and after a few years he was reincarnated as a monk who fled Tibet during the Chinese invasion, settling a few miles from where we stand.

These reincarnations, or *tulku*s, are common still. Enlight-ened lamas, they return to earth by their own will to guide the Buddhist faithful.

But as we climb the wooden stairs to a chamber above the prayer hall, where the Ceremony of Long Life is swelling with drums and horns, the abbot's talk falters around this *tulku*. Scandalously the monk had married, then become a tantric yogi, and under the abbot's guarded words I wonder if the *tulku* had been a little mad. 'He wanted to re-create the monastery he had lost near Kailas – the Chinese had destroyed it by then – but he was poor, and . . . sickness prevented it. But before he died, he left a mandala describing where the new monastery should be built. And it was on this spot.'

We settle at a heavy table that looks as if it has been here centuries. The abbot says: 'So his son founded this monastery with a handful of monks in 1985. He is still here, the oldest man in our monastery, and afterwards the *tulku*'s own grandson became the divine incarnation, and is here too, studying as a monk.'

I listen in silence, perplexed by this unearthly genealogy. (Later I glimpsed the old founder, mounting ceremoniously to his room after the Service of Long Life.) The abbot recounts these reincarnations as matter-of-factly as natural births. There are five *tulku*s among his own monks, he says, reincarnated from different lama ancestors.

I stare at him across a deep divide. He has the moon face of Tibetan calm, regular and stressless, its lips upturned faintly like those of a statued Buddha. These reincarnations to him are conduits of an enlightenment that springs like a flame from candle to candle, man to man (they are almost always men). The precise nature of the flame, the continuance – psyche, spirit, memory – is uncertain, but the *tulku*, as its holder, is the envoy of a changeless purity.

The abbot senses the doubt in me, I think. He orders a novice to bring us tea, while I shift uncomfortably on the monastic bench. He is less than half my age, yet his surety is grand and a little mysterious. But I belong helplessly to another culture. He is focused on spiritual continuance, while I am overborne by individual death. What is it, I ask, that survives to be reincarnated?

Some shadowy capacity for remembrance must endure, the abbot implies, because of the way a *tulku* is discovered. When a likely child is located, a group of monastic elders confronts him with various possessions, and the infant is acknowledged if he recognises those of his *tulku* predecessor. This practice, or something like it, has perhaps been going on in Tibet since the twelfth century, and reached its zenith in the recognition of the reincarnate Dalai Lamas. The process was often corrupt, of course. But sometimes, as now, it seemed that Tibet's heart survived in these sacred kinships, flowing through generations like divine electricity, or simply – like this monastery itself – as stupendous acts of remembrance.

'But our life is very hard,' the abbot says. 'Some monks cannot take it too long. Many leave for Kathmandu, or join our monasteries down on the plains or in India. Or they marry.' He adds regretfully, courteously: 'The West is attractive to many of them.' Even on his own wrist, I notice, the prayer beads nestle beside a digital watch. 'So our problems always vary. A few years ago the Maoists threatened all this region. They closed down many monasteries and forced the monks into working as farmers. They even captured two of our own community.'

I wonder aloud what happened. The monasteries were cruelly vulnerable, no longer armed fraternities as they had once been.

The abbot smiles ironically. 'The two monks went separate ways. One escaped and went to India. The other was converted by the Maoists, and carried their secret messages through the mountains. After the Maoists made peace with the government, he went back to his village and got married. We never saw him again.'

Marriage haunts monastic life. There is little compensating comfort. In the old Tibet the monks had been a pampered elite among serf farmers and nomads. But here, in a Hindu land, the rigours of their life are untainted by any vestige of wealth. They are sidelined, isolated, perhaps cleansed. The abbot's own grandfather, he says, had been a lama in Tibet, but lapsed and married. 'Then the Chinese invaded our country, and my father left home and fled.' He breaks off. 'The Chinese killed many of us last year, you know. I don't hate the Chinese people, but their policies, their government . . .' He bows his head. 'It was my father who taught me the sacred scriptures and our country's history. And when I was eleven I decided to become a monk.'

'So young!'

But even here the novices were boys as young as nine – some seventy of them – whose adolescence waited like a time bomb. He goes on: 'But when I told my parents, my mother cried "No! No! Not a monk! You will just sit there, studying", and even my father said: "You may want to go now, but when you are twenty, twenty-five, you will regret it, you will want to leave and marry." I was the first son, you see, and the first son is meant to look after his parents. All the same, I went away.' In the hall beneath us, the monks' prayers have softened to purring. 'Now I cannot help them. I am here. They are far down the valley.' He pulls his crimson robes closer about his neck.

I ask bleakly: 'How do they live?'

'Their second son is twenty-five now, and he looks after them.'

'Do they want to return to Tibet?'

'They cannot.'

The people of this region, he says, can obtain a Chinese permit to cross the border for a week, usually to trade, and may with luck extend it for a pilgrimage to Kailas. But few of them did; and the monks were too afraid. 'It is you who can go to Kailas,' he says. He has never been. He says this without bitterness, yet the few Western trekkers passing through have motives alien to any he knows. As for my own, I hesitate to speak them to him, inchoate as they are. They belong to a world grown dim to him, to Western self and attachment, not to the abstract compassion that he entertains. He speaks of Kailas with a dreamlike evangelism. He wants me to honour the journey that he cannot make himself.

'You know this is a mountain of great power. To travel there multiplies merit. The Buddha often flew there with his followers. And spiritual treasure-seekers meditated there

– thousands of them – so its caves are full of blessing.' Sometimes I cannot decide whether he is a sage or a child. And
often his words are drowned by the pounding drums
beneath us. 'People walk around the mountain to cleanse
their evil, the ten seats of sin. Yes, they may also come
because they want things, perhaps success in some business,
perhaps they have too many daughters and want a son . . .'

After a while, when the sound below subsides, he gets
up and we descend to the prayer hall. The monks are
dispersing in flocks of crimson and saffron, and the
temple darkens.

He takes me round a dim confusion. The avenue of low
pews, where the monks had sat among cushions and bells,
leads to the painted skeleton of a great altar. It rises in tiers
of bright artefacts: offerings in barley dough and wax,
guttering butter-lamps and bowls of water, plastic flowers,
monstrances, peacock feathers, topped by photographs of
prestigious lamas in ceremonial crowns and dark glasses.
Above these again a huge gilded Buddha, draped unrecog-
nisably in golden cloth, gazes from his halo with a smile of
exalted absence. The abbot, patient and soft-voiced, guides
me along the walls, identifying statues of other Buddhas and
teachers, goddesses and multiple bodhisattvas, the blessed
ones who postpone their own nirvana for the salvation
of the world. In this proliferating pantheon, often elusive
to me, the deities may reappear in different aspects or
emanations of themselves. Their arms and faces divide and
multiply in the dark. Often they turn feral and demonic.
They hold up gems and lotuses, rosaries and thunderbolts,
and stare into nothing. They are not only gods, but incarnate

ideas. Their gestures are a cryptic language. Here divinity is protean and fluid. It manifests in bestial fury, female pity; it wears a smile of compassion and a garland of skulls. The abbot leads me falteringly on. But often I can discern no more than the gilded hand of a body obscured by votive scarves, or the plaster grimace of a demon. Most of the images are so coarsely moulded that I cannot imagine any sanctity or meaning in them.

The doors close behind us, dimming the last light. I am uneasily aware of walking among a revered army whose evolution the Buddha would have condemned. The Buddhism that Tibet first received in the seventh century – more than a thousand years after the death of its founder – was already rich in these alternately beautiful and grotesque offspring. Moreover the faith created its Tibetan bridgehead in the isolated kingdom of Shang-shung, near Mount Kailas, and in those bitter plateaux encountered a swarm of chthonic gods and spirits who violently coloured it. Then, over the coming centuries, the richly evolved Mahayana tradition of northern India infused the whole land, bringing with it a generous field of salvation and a host of variegated Buddhas, bodhisattvas and Hindu deities in disguise.

Of this inclusive pantheon the figures around me are descendants. Here is Chenresig, the Tibetan form of Avalokitesvara, whose incarnation is the Dalai Lama. He is the all-seeing lord of compassion, whose myriad arms burst like a peacock's tail behind him, each hand pierced with an eye. The abbot points out the god's offspring, Drolma, the kindly goddess of pity and fertility, and several obscure incarnations of Padmasambhava, Tibet's patron saint.

In these, and the figures crowding round them, the austere origins of Buddhism are transformed. What was once a rigorous, agnostic philosophy, in which karma persisted through countless generations, has evolved into the promise of swift, esoteric systems of liberation, guiding saviours. It was in Tibet that tantric Buddhism reached its apogee, initiating its devotees into practices that enabled them to bypass the toilsome cycle of worldly reincarnations and enter nirvana in a lifetime's leap.

His monastery, the abbot says, belongs to the sect of Nyingma, the Ancient Ones, who claim their origins in Tibet's oldest Buddhism. They are followers, above all, of tantric ritual and contemplation, and at the end the abbot leads me, as if in challenge, to two statues in towering embrace. Here is the white-painted Buddha Vajrasattva — shiny, crude, abstract. In his circling arms clings a sinuous consort, her legs hooked around his waist, their loins inter-meshed. This is not sex as humans know it, but a marriage of symbols. They suggest eternal orgasm. Their nudity is glorified by bangles and tiaras. Her mouth is raised to his impersonal lips in an exalted offering of life.

The abbot says: 'This is the union of nothing and com-passion.'

'Nothing?'

'The god is nothing. He realises nothingness.' The abbot is voicing the insistent wisdom of the Mahayana: the asser-tion that phenomena do not in themselves exist, that all is relative, illusion.

'And she?'

'She is compassion. She completes him.'

Such figures of carnal bliss generate many interpretations, and among advanced adepts their visualisation, even their enactment, may achieve a mystic dissolution on the path to Buddha-hood. Sometimes compassion is attributed to the man, and wisdom – flashing insight – to the woman. Often she is conceived as his *shakti,* his embodied energy, entwining the god who created her.

There are married lamas, the abbot says, who follow this sexual path, but not in his monastery. In the past, tantric extremes were often the way of solitary yogis, but in the monasteries the tantra coexists with philosophy and dialectics. However fractured since the golden fourteenth and fifteenth centuries, these parallel traditions of logic and lived mysticism endure. On the banked shelves along the temple walls the abbot locates the cloth-enveloped scriptures of the Buddha's supposed sayings and their commentaries – the Kangyur and the Tengyur – which in old Tibet inspired a vast and subtle literature of metaphysics. Here too are the tantric texts beloved of the abbot's order. He talks of them with easy affection, while I remain baffled. Who was the primordial Buddha Samantabhadra? What is the Secret Essence Tantra? How to understand the Clear Light of the Great Perfection? They rise from a sacred learning of which barely a fraction has been translated.

Only one element in these secret disciplines is half familiar to me. Forty years ago an old friend, the traveller Freya Stark, had given me a mandala of symmetrically disposed Buddhas on a golden field. She had bought this in Nepal, drawn to its strangeness. To me its cloud-enthroned Buddhas resembled autocratic babies mysteriously afloat; but once perhaps they had accompanied the meditation of a monk or hermit as his private window on salvation.

Classically such mandalas portray a deity seated at the heart of a densely walled palace. The picture acts like a sac-red domain, impermeable to the illusory world outside. Adepts often use the mandala to focus on the deity with whom they strive to identify. Jung thought it a healing archetype of the unconscious. Other adepts use it more lightly as an aide-memoir. Still others systematically imagine their mandala to be centred on Mount Meru or Kailas, the spine of the world, and their own bodies aligned with the mountain too, drawing down power from above.

In the temple porch the abbot points out a muralled mandala whose archetype was designed in legend by the Buddha himself. 'This is the original, the Wheel of Becoming. You see it is turned by the god of death, Yama. And in the centre . . . people falling.'

I stare up. Around the axis of this great spoked disc, an arc of humans is climbing toward nirvana or catapulting down to hell. At their core, isolated on the wheel's hub, I make out the tableau of a serpent, a cockerel and a pig biting each other's tails.

'These are the poisons at the world's heart,' the abbot says. 'The snake-one is anger, the pig-one is ignorance, the cock is desire. You see . . .'

I see that in the rest of the wheel all mortality is going about its business: conversing, acquiring, making love. Only the Buddha stands outside the circle, pointing to the moon in sign of liberation. But his nirvana, of course, cannot be depicted; even the hell at the wheel's base looks schematic and unlikely; and the lives of those trapped on this earthly roundabout appear innocent, sometimes a little comic. If the artist was trying to suggest suffering, he seems to have lost heart. The animals that represent brutishness stand tranquil as if in paradise, and the gods – who will come to grief in time – are enjoying themselves in the interim.

I ask the abbot what monk or layman painted this schema. (The role of the painter in Tibetan life is as disputed as most else.)

'Painting is a tradition among our monks,' he says. 'An old man who fled with the Dalai Lama taught it here, but went away to meditate in a cave near Kermi, and died there. He had already taught a disciple, but that monk left for Simikot' – he smiles forgivingly – 'and went into business. But he in turn had taught two others . . .'

'And who painted the Wheel of Becoming?'

'I'm not sure.' The abbot's clear brows knit for a second, then he laughs. 'But I think it was the businessman.'

On the track beyond the monastery I come upon two memorial towers in rough stone. I peer through the narrow openings into their core, cluttered with pebbles and dust. Here relatives place a little rice or even a fleck of gold, or insert paper mantras to Drolma, the goddess of compassion. Deep inside I see the tiny cones moulded out of clay and a pounded fragment of bone from whoever is remembered here.

In these valleys, where bodies are burned or fed to vultures, the vanishment of the dead seems utter. Only the rare turret or stupa of some revered lama makes a gesture at remembrance. But when I ask a group of passing monks about the towers – when were they built, who do they commemorate? – they do not know. And why would they care, who have been taught the transience of things?

As they walk on, I wonder at them, their lightness, their lack of need. They might already have passed through a painless, premature death. They have shed what others shed in dying. They will leave nothing material behind them to be divided, claimed or loved. Their dispossession strikes me as at once freedom, and a poignant depletion. Their buoyant laughter follows me up the valley, but I do not quite envy them. I only wonder with a muffled pang what it would be in the West to step outside the chain of bequeathal and inheritance, as they do, until human artefacts mean nothing at all.

My feet slow on the trail. But my memories come too hard for quiet thought. With the death of a last parent, material things – old correspondence, a dilapidated house, a pair of slippers – emerge like orphans to enshrine the dead. My mother threw away nothing. Her drawers spilt out letters, diaries, documents, photos, fifty, seventy, eighty years old, with the stacked correspondence of my father, my dead sister, my nurse, even my nurse's mother. For months the papers lie piled, waiting. They grow huge with delayed sadness. How to decide what is to survive, what is to perish? The value of things no longer belongs to cost or beauty, but only to memory. The chipped and faded teacup is more precious than the silver tray that nobody used. And the letters bring confusion. Sometimes what was written for a day echoes in your head as if for ever. Every one discarded

sounds a tiny knell of loss. The past drops away into the
waste-paper basket and oblivion, and in this monstrous
disburdening, grief returns you to a kind of childish
dependence. You sift and preserve (for whom?) and cling to
trivia. You have become the guardian of their past, even its
recreator.

I had planned to burn my parents' love letters, then find
I cannot. Instead I start to read, guiltily, fearfully, as if
testing water. I have an idea that they should survive, placed
in some archive, perhaps to flow at last unmoored into
history. I tie them with new rubber bands – the old ones
have corroded over the envelopes – and stack them away,
I do not know for what. This, I suppose, is how once-
private things endure: not by intention, but because their
extinction is unbearable. So I dither between keeping and
destroying – both seem like betrayal – and I store the letters,
in all their devotion, their longing and sometimes loneliness, until another time.

In my father's wartime letters censorship precludes any
word of military activity. He surrounds this void with casual incident, humour and remarks on flowers and birds.
Even from the shell-racked beachhead of Anzio his letters
tell my mother that April violets and wild crocus are growing there, with vetches, scarlet pimpernels and orchids. His
caravan at divisional headquarters, he writes, is adorned
with photographs of her, my sister and myself, among walls
of cigarette tins stuffed with irises and cyclamen. There are
birds too ('but of course not many owing to the continual
explosions') – yellowhammers and nightingales, which sing
by day, and 'the prettiest is a wren-like little bird rather like

a goldfinch', which reminds him of her. Only obliquely does he mention the shell craters around him, or the death of fellow officers, or – months later – how his caravan (and our photographs) was shredded by shrapnel.

Sometimes the darkened world and wasted years seem only a tunnel to the dream light of reunion. But their mutual danger went on haunting them. During the Blitz my mother had driven trucks in the London docks. Then my father begins to mention the Russian advance, and the Wehrmacht's decline. ('Our prisoners are poor fellows compared to those we captured in Tunis.') As the war nears its end, the scent of pines in the Italian hills starts to remind him of India, and on VE Day anemones and sorrel are whitening in the Austrian woods. He had not seen my mother for over two and a half years.

We are standing on a railway station in Hampshire, my hand in hers. My sister Carol is on her other side, I think. I am barely seven years old. At school I have announced that my father has killed all the Germans and is coming home to put up the Christmas decorations, in May. And now the steam train has pulled in, and returning servicemen are flooding down the platform. I scan their faces in paralysed suspense. I cannot remember what my father looks like. The men approaching us have alien moustaches and shining boots. Then a staff cane comes somersaulting out of a carriage window and my mother cries: 'That will be him! He's always joking.' The next moment he is striding towards us. My mother's hands loosen in ours. He is almost six foot five, huge for his day, unreachably handsome and covered in medals. And he is suffused with happiness. He is the father every schoolboy wants. I am at once scared and elated. When we arrive home my rediscovered parents do not reach the sitting room but fall embracing on the spare bed off the hall. Carol and I watch in stunned surprise, then enfold each other in copycat confusion.

I close the letters up, with the photo albums that my father kept even before his marriage. In his earliest, Indian snapshots the young officers go unnamed. But who were the women, I wonder, left behind in sepia faintness, labelled 'Diana' or 'Marjorie'? Or the merry flapper who inscribed above her photograph in parting: 'Good luck, old thing'? He never spoke of them. He liked to imagine, my mother said, that there had been nobody before her.

But in my mother's first snapshots she is no more than a tiny girl; in my father's he is a twenty-year-old cadet; and for seven years of marriage the camera records a carefree childlessness. Around these early albums – for their leftover child – something subtly shifts. The couple who inhabit them lived before I existed. They are young again, far younger than I am now, and a little mysterious. She kneels among her Dalmatian puppies or rides her horse in an army point-to-point. He is buffooning at the regimental party, dressed as a conjuror. They live in roles and contexts where I no longer miss them, and this separateness assuages mourning. They inhabit their own lives, and I lose them a little. The tall lieutenant jokes with his comrades five years before he met my mother, fifteen before I was born. You recognise at last that their lives were not yours.

Yet strangely, in all but the youngest photos, the opposite is also true. Somehow, as if they possessed precognition or you were seeing them bifocally, they are already your parents, already senior, and inexplicably, although blithely young, are forever older than you.

All day a wind has been whipping up the Karnali valley, and intensifies at evening as we approach Yangar. From a distance the village might be built of card houses. They mount on one another's shoulders precipitously above the river, until they merge with living rock, flat-roofed and raised in horizontal courses of timber and stones, their flag-poles streaming prayers into the wind. Women are washing clothes where a brook splashes down, and turn their oval faces to us, smiling. We might already be in Tibet. We tramp the labyrinthine lanes under blank walls and beetling eaves. Serried beam-ends poke out like tiers of cannon. The houses loom in an interlocking maze of shifting levels and walkways. The alleys are twilit ravines. All around us long ladders climb and descend to aerial yards and terraces, and the voices of invisible people sound from the sky.

These dizzy perspectives multiply even after a family invites us in. The Dendu Lamas are farming people with short, Tibetan faces and ebony eyes. Yet they inhabit the air. In these eyries a woman may emerge to chat from the door of a terrace two yards away, but between you yawns a thirty-foot drop into the street. The heads of horses apparently stabled underground gaze into lanes at first-storey level. You ascend three tiers only to find yourself on somebody else's ground floor, and cowbells jangle from what you imagined to be an attic. Nobody can afford to sleepwalk. Dhabu sits down by mistake on a rickety balustrade, and is nearly pitched, laughing hysterically, into the alley below.

Dendu, our host, is forty and spry. He wears Western dress like all the village men – anoraks and shabby trousers made in China – and a peaked cap blazoned 'Life Plus'. His big, loose mouth gives him a deceptive air of languor. We scale a series of ladders – giddy flights of notched tree trunks – and stoop into rooms whose deep-framed windows leak in a dead, sunless light. Their floors, ceilings and pillars are all of heavy sal wood, where the dents of axe and chisel still show, but embedded now to a sombre, burnished strength. Dendu says his father built this ancient-seeming keep. Its pillars drive down two or three floors to the rock, and its beams are patterned with white circles native to Tibet. It was built for stocky mountaineers. Its furniture is thick and dwarfish. I bang my head on the door lintels. The low table looks like a bench, and the blundering Westerner sits down on it. Tolerantly Dendu motions to the floor, and in the faded light we sit in a genial circle round their stove, where his wife bakes bread. She is too shy at first to speak. Her jet-black hair parts into pigtails round high-coloured cheekbones. The shelves behind her are banked with gleaming tins and thermoses, a clock and a gutted radio, and hung with polished ladles. She hands out milk fresh from their cow. Beside her a bridal cupboard in Pompeian red is limned with faded flowers. She slaps the dough between her hands, on and on, then smoothes it on the hob to brown into thin bread, while Dendu pounds pickles in a wooden mortar.

Their village shares the dilemma of all this region, he says. Their land yields a single crop of barley each year, and it's not enough to feed them. So every spring and autumn he loads illicitly felled pine trees on to his three yaks and leads them north over the border into timber-starved Tibet. The town of Taklakot, he says, is the centre for this common contraband. Then he returns south carrying Chinese clothes for sale, with shoes, beer and flour.

I think of the poverty-stricken Thakuri villages far down the valley – of Lauri and his ragged children – and wonder where Dendu's children are. At first I imagine he has none. His wife, in their arranged marriage, is six years older than him. But Dendu is a fixer. His clever daughters have entered the rumbustious boarding school downriver, then gone on to a charity school in Dharamsala, home in exile of the Dalai Lama. And his cherished son has won assistance to a college in Kathmandu, from which he will return to them. These despised Bhotia, it seems, are turning their isolation to account in trade – 'China is nearer to us than Kathmandu,' Dendu says – while exploiting their Tibetan heritage. 'Things are all right for us.' He offers us tea mixed with salt and yak butter. 'Things are good.'

But what happens, I wonder, to families denied a son?

Dendu says: 'Then their daughter must bring her husband from his village to live with them. It may be far away – nobody marries within the village. But nobody marries outside their caste either. Unless it is for love.'

Love. It is not much spoken of. A bride must leave her childhood home without this tenderness. Years ago I had come upon the corpse of a young woman floating in the

Cauvery river in India. The police had shrugged her away. It was only a woman, they said. She had probably been broken by her husband's home.

Tentatively I ask Dendu's wife about this ordeal. What had she felt?

Dendu answers for her at once, but kindly: 'That is our way in this country.'

But I ask her again, tactlessly. She shrinks behind the stove and her face disappears into her hands. At last she whispers: 'The first three years were very hard. My village is far away. I thought about my parents all the time.' Then a high, smothered tinkling sounds through her splayed fingers. I am afraid that she is crying, but it is laughter. She looks up. 'Then my love for my husband came, and there were children.' She smiles, as if with remembered relief. He is smiling too, suddenly embarrassed. She starts slapping the dough between her palms again, while he pokes sticks into the stove.

Sometimes silence falls: not the awkward Western hiatus, but a comfortable interval festive with burps and chomping, among people to whom eating is not taken for granted. Immured in the dark comfort of their home, in this scarred magnificence of wood, I momentarily forget Dendu's tree-felling, and lapse into drowsy well-being. Their welcome is warm and modest. She shows little jewellery, but wears the striped apron and long skirts of Tibet. Their larder is stored with rice and gas canisters. They share the same wide, calm face.

Their faith is far removed from the monastery downriver. Two temples – male and female – hang in the crags above the village, but Dendu does not know why they were gendered. 'That's just what we call them.' A few times a year the villagers assemble to pray in one or other. They speak to no god or Buddha in particular, he says. They just pray for their good fortune. And on a plateau further upriver, their bodies after death are cut in pieces. 'We used to tip bodies into the river,' he says, 'but not now. Now it is cleaner. The birds come.'

From their rooftop in the starlight the temples appear only as high, empty spaces pale with prayer flags. After Dendu retires for the night in their storeroom, and Dhabu to his horse, Iswor, Ram and I lie in our chrysalid sleeping bags along the floor, lit by a naked bulb. Outside is silence. But Ram has nightmares beside me, his teeth grinding, his scooped-out cheeks turned to mahogany, so that I wonder whether to wake him, but do not, and he moans at last into quiet.

CHAPTER FIVE

. . . .

From far up our path, Yangar remains in sight, and stirring with the dawn. Momentarily we stop and look back on the illusion of a golden valley. For a mile the cliff walls ease apart on its enclosed peace, and the first sunlight is trickling through the fields. A tributary stream glitters down across our way, and birds are shifting in the wild apricot trees.

Then we turn and move on high above the river. Far ahead, beyond its long, constricted passage, the white palisade of mountains bars our skyline, and a few clouds rise like smoke signals from its peaks. But the fluting of the *optatus* (or *saturatus*) cuckoo still echoes down the valley, and a handsome fox saunters blithely across our path. It is hard to remember that the fields of Yangar, spread like magic in the young light, are too poor to support their farmers' lives. Somewhere far off, faint in the stillness, sounds the ring of an axe.

The valley is closing in. Below us outsize trees still crowd along the river – sometimes the spruces rise 150 feet from its banks – but we are tramping high up through thinning scrub and rock. Cistus and cream-coloured potentilla flower everywhere; flights of yellow-breasted wagtails are about, and a startling trogon precedes us from branch to branch in flashes of crimson and black. But now we are crossing the ever-wider track of avalanches, whose torn-up rocks have stilled to minefields of razor scree. The few trees are dwindling from our trail. Often the pines stand erect, but blackened and long dead, as if burnt from within, and sometimes the cliffs of the river bank opposite descend near vertically for 500 feet.

Then our trail drops to the river. Steel cables carry us over a thin plank bridge, and we mount the far side at last to the scattered houses of Muchu. High on its hill a tiny old man in spectacles is trying to rotate the bald prayer drum in the temple porch, while a frail-looking monk struggles up the slope to unlock its doors. I do not know what to expect. Compared to the monastery complex near Yalbang, the temple is small and solitary. What could have survived in this wilderness, overrun for years by atheist partisans?

The doors open on dereliction. In the pallor falling from a narrow skylight, we are walking not into ransacked disorder but a scene of helpless decay. The temple must have fallen desolate piecemeal, over years of neglect. Framed by rough pillars and low, makeshift tables, its altar is a rotting shelf where a line of butter lamps burnt out long ago. In the wall behind, the niches gape empty or glower with blackened figurines that I cannot decipher. A cascade of soiled ceremonial scarves dangles from the foremost statues, whose stucco faces of pink and gold grin out in ruin. In other niches the holy scriptures are piled in confusion, and Padmasambhava sits surrounded by his wives, all drunkenly aslant. Everywhere the paint is peeling or gone, and at the centre, in a crimson alcove aswirl with faded dragons, Chenresig, the Tibetan god of mercy, towers over a photograph of the scandalous *tulku* reincarnation whose story I had heard at Yalbang, and who died in this village.

The monk has padded after us, with the old man whirling his own prayer wheel. The statue of Chenresig, he murmurs, was discovered miraculously in a nearby river; the others the villagers made with their own hands. I can discern no difference. Chenresig's golden head bulges with blank eyes. His raised hand dribbles strings of amulets and old coins. Other statues are crammed together in pious anarchy, waving tridents or cradling bowls. What power they might once have owned has blurred to a shared corrosion, as if they were starting to revert to the chalk from which they came.

I ask the monk how old this temple is, but he does not know. There are eighteen monks in the village, he says, and they take turns tending the temple. 'When the Maoists came, we formed a committee of villagers, and they left us alone.'

'The police ran away.' The old man fixes me with cloudless eyes. 'But we banded together' – he motions at the altar – 'and saved everything.'

I am not seeing the shrine as they are, I know. For them this derelict barn is a place of redemption, cleansed by its crossfire of gazing Buddhas. Only Iswor mutters: 'How poor . . . how poor . . .'

On the walls, the damp stucco is bellying out and the murals falling in wholesale chunks. The Buddhas of the Past, Present and Future levitate across the dark in green haloes and thickets of painted roses, but are peeling away. Even Yama, the lord of death, is dimming in the plaster to the transience he himself ordains, together with the demon counterparts of kindlier gods.

These so-called wrathful deities infiltrate the Tibetan pantheon with terror. The old man's prayer wheel spins faster when he passes one. For some reason here they look more threatening in decay than when complete. They haunt every temple like a bitter shadow world. Some are mundane spirits with specialist powers, demanding tribute; others have been coopted as guardians of the Buddhist law. But most prominent are the alter egos of benign bodhisattvas, who don awesome forms to fight ignorance and evil. It is as if these saints had exploded out of tranquil repression into insensate fury. They throw away their lotuses and begging bowls and snatch up cleavers and flaying knives. Their eyes swell from peaceful slivers to jutting orbs, and their once-folded legs break free into stomping columns that squash Hindu gods underfoot. Sometimes they put on living serpents and tiger skins, and their brows sprout tiaras of skulls. Their jewellery is human bones. One and all, their mouths gape open on flame-like tongues and rows of feral teeth that end in wicked little tusks. Some are still attached to their consorts, who have turned vicious and unsexed.

The interpretation of these monsters is conflicted. Classically they are said to echo abstract forces as surely as their serene counterparts, and liberate those who realise their truth. Even Yama – who rampages bull-faced and pitch black in a halo of fire and demons – is only an emanation of the merciful bodhisattva Avalokitesvara. But other scholars believe these inverted gods are psychic reactions to a harsh landscape and brutal cold; while yet others claim that they are the shamanic leftovers of an older Tibet, still vengeful and unassimilated.

The number and power of such divinities is echoed in the demon-ridden life of everyday Tibet. But the origins of the most formidable are not found there at all, but in the warm plains and tantric texts of India. The Hindu god Shiva himself, who meditates eternally on the summit of Mount Kailas, finds his savage mirror image in his own consort, Kali.

In the dark valley of Dakshinkali, south of Kathmandu, the Hindu goddess has her sanctuary where two rivers meet. Every Saturday, pilgrims in their hundreds circle down the wooded gorge to feed her. Women mostly, brilliant in their best saris, carry split coconuts, marigolds, and cockerels with trussed legs. Often they lead unwary goats, and even buffaloes. The sounds of celebration rise from the valley: chattering cries and laughter, broken chanting, the clash of bells. Holy men inscribe the pilgrims' foreheads with *tika*s of rice and vermilion; cooking fires flicker on the terraces. As I descend, the pilgrims slow to a clamorous queue, and I glimpse on the valley floor an open temple dripping with maroon hangings and overarched by four gilded serpents.

At first I imagine that the crimson coating on the basrelief of Kali is moving drapery. Then I see the carving is awash with blood. In this inner courtyard, where the worshippers cram shoulder to shoulder, the casual priests, their robes hitched to the thigh, receive their platters of hibiscus and marigold, while two butchers collar the living beasts. Beneath the bloodied goddess, the goats collapse at the slash of a knife, and the cockerels' heads are flipped off like bottle tops. The sculptured face shows only slit eyes and the mouth of a spoilt girl. A severed buffalo head sits like a gory anvil at her feet, its carcass foundered to the ground a yard away. A guardian yells at me to remove my shoes. The marble floors are a sea of blood and offal. The lissom women walk here barefoot, like priestesses. Bells crash and tinkle as they circle the shrine. Grey mongrels sleep underfoot, oblivious on the crimsoned tiles.

Kali's statue is one of those primitive images the more potent for their inhuman muteness. Classically she is portrayed hideous, a trampler of demons and a drunkard on blood. At Dakshinkali she accepts for sacrifice only uncastrated males. Shiva alone can control her. In yogic practice he represents pure, inert consciousness, she the energy by which he creates. In other guises she becomes a figure of cosmic triumph, the bringer of change who at last devours time itself and lapses back into primal dark. Sometimes she is even described as beautiful.

I climb back up the valley, where families are feasting on their sacrifices under the trees. Everyone is in high spirits except me, hypocritically repelled by what Western abattoirs conceal. Along the path the stalls are selling trinkets and fluffy toys: little teddy bear pendants and animal heads with Disney smiles.

That evening, in my monastery guest house in Kathmandu, I peeled off my blood-soaked socks and sat in the garden where the marigolds and hibiscus bloomed unpicked. Tashi, a monk who had befriended me, sat opposite and listened to Kali's slaughter with disgust. He came from a poor village in Bhutan. The Buddhist ban on taking life had long ago sickened him of bloodshed, and the wrathful deities in his own Buddhist pantheon had calmed into saviours.

'There's a Hindu goddess has her festival here in September,' he said. 'Kali or Durga, I don't know. The streets stream with blood for three days. In past years the king started the festival by slaughtering something. And we monks hate this. People sacrifice in the hope of better business deals or male children. How can they promote themselves through the suffering of poor animals? We always close ourselves away for those days, and light lamps for the souls of the animals and pray.'

In Tashi's monastery, a month before, I had watched a monk reaching out to the folding gate of a storeroom. Gently from its interstices, which would crush together when the door closed, he extracted a small marbled butterfly, and carried it away to a flower.

Tashi had a soft, peasant face and crescent mouth. He was only thirty but would soon begin the three-year period of solitary meditation that he craved. 'This animal slaughter will stop in the end,' he said. 'Young people will change it. They are turning against the practices of their elders. Everything is changing . . .'

I forgot that he himself was young. Under his loose magenta robes his arms showed smooth, hairless, but his face was blotched and scarred by his rural childhood, and seemed settled now into a sturdy peace. 'How they will replace those practices I don't know. We live in an age of decline. I think before the Chinese invaded Tibet, and our Buddhist people were dispersed, that our faith was much purer. Now we're exposed to Western ways, and of course to women. In our faith a senior monk – one who's achieved a certain level of realisation – may sometimes marry. So she becomes an inspiration to him, and he a guru to her. But this is rare, and late. And now I hear of young monks going after girls, and some Western women complain that monks grab at them. The monks see women on television, of course . . .'

I asked with vague surprise: 'They watch much television?'

'Oh yes, a lot. The monks get very excited.' He was starting to laugh. 'Only last night all the monks got *furious*.'

'Why was that?' But I knew their calm could be deceptive. In Tibet they remained the spearhead of political protest, and centuries ago the monasteries had run amok in internecine war.

'It was Manchester United. All the monks love football. They got very angry last night about the European Cup. Manchester United were beaten by Barcelona, and all the monks love Manchester United. You should see them from behind, watching television, how they argue. They thought the referee was biased . . . they were enraged how he gave out penalty tickets. They started shouting things.'

I shook my head. 'I thought the monks prayed in the evening.'

'Well, perhaps it's a kind of meditation. They concentrate on the ball and the rest of the world goes away . . .'

* * *

In the valley below Muchu, the Karnali river bends suddenly north through impassable gorges, and will rejoin our track only on the Tibetan frontier. Meanwhile Iswor points us to where the tributary of Kumuchhiya falls steeply from the west. On the ridge beyond Muchu we pass a mani wall and a chorten – one of those stupa-like cenotaphs that Tibetan peoples cherish – and reach a half-derelict police post. The site had been abandoned to Maoist guerrillas long ago, but for two years now a twelve-man police squad from Kathmandu had reluctantly returned: slight, dark men, isolated and perhaps a little afraid. A wary sergeant scans our permits and sends us on.

We go steeply down. Log bridges carry us to the tributary's north bank. It is almost noon. The land is stripped of trees. The river whitens far ahead of us, splaying round stranded boulders. Only patches of scrub hold to the nearer hills, which have often eroded to whorls of naked rock, and the shale makes yellow forks against the mountains.

As our path steepens up the valley, Iswor asks: 'How are you feeling?' He sounds concerned. 'Are you okay?'

Yes, so far I am. But I listen to my body now. Old wounds gently remind me of themselves, like voices echoing: a knee cartilage damaged since boyhood, an ankle ligament torn in Syria, a fractured spine from a road accident. They return only in nudges and twinges, but I recognise them with suppressed unease: who would evacuate us out of these hills?

I tell myself and Iswor: 'I'm fine. *Absolutely fine,*' and for some reason we laugh.

✳ ✳ ✳

The journey does not nurture reflection, as I once hoped. The going is too hard, too steep. Every footstep on the stone-littered track needs a tiny, half-conscious decision, and brings its attrition unnoticed. Only in dreamlike intervals, perched on a rock while Iswor rests his load, can I imagine the path as oddly intimate to me, like a memory trace.

You look back down the valley and wonder: how did I come so far? A few minutes ago, or perhaps an hour, you passed a trader's shelter – a sheepskin draped between rocks – and now it has dwindled to a fleck below you. Perhaps, after all, you have walked this path unawares, drugged by the rhythm of your boots, as if dreaming, and only a passage of startling beauty or hardship wrenched you awake. In this thinning air you even imagine you may be nearing the end. But the speechless white mountain ahead is not Kailas, of course. Kailas, in your reverie, hangs like a stage prop out of sight, waiting. As the crow flies it is barely fifty miles away: but in another country, another ether.

To Hindus, 'departure for Kailas' is a metaphor for death.

A young Tibetan monk from Yalbang overtakes us, making for Taklakot, where he will buy Chinese shoes for his monastery. He is travelling fast, in plain clothes, without a passport. He is buoyant and sure. He will slip past the border guards incognito, he says, no problem. But among the rough traders along the way he looks innocent and placeless, as if nothing has ever touched him. He wears a bobble hat and carries a furled umbrella. He left his home long ago, he says, and walked to the Yalbang monastery. 'Compared to my teacher, I love my parents only a little now.' He signals this dwindled affection with two narrowing fingers, and smiles. 'My teacher is my true father.' After a while he strides ahead alone along the mountain, singing with mysterious merriment. You might imagine he comes from a land free of evil. Travellers have always marvelled at the Tibetans' light hearts, as they think them. As long ago as the tenth century the Arab geographer Masudi wrote of a people beyond the Himalayas who laughed even in bereavement.

The monk shrinks to a dot ahead of me. He has taken Iswor with him, talking cheerily, and I see them ascending farther and farther where the track dissolves into the debris of an avalanche. By the time I reach it they are high above me, still climbing. Its petrified flood has become our stairway upwards. Its rocks look raw and new, as if the carapace of the mountain had been ripped open in a vertical wound. For hours, it seems, I am toiling upwards. The stones shift and grate underfoot. My body no longer seems quite my own. The landslide is so long and steep that I dare not look up for its end. Instead I fix my eyes on a boulder fifty yards away, perhaps, and reach it like a swimmer in a storm. For long minutes I am slumped on rocks, gasping, my legs gone. I turn my back and stare down at the distant river and flayed hills, calming my heart, wondering why I am doing this, before standing upright and starting again. Now the rock fall seems to be pushing physically against me. The sun blazes above. I start counting my steps, and even the stones under my feet: grey, cinnamon red, intricately veined. Then my trekking pole snaps in the shale. I think: if things are like this at 11,000 feet, how will they be at over 18,500, where I am going? Now, for fear of losing heart at the gully opening ahead, I barely lift my gaze from the rocks a step in front of me.

Colin Thubron

Slowly I am invaded by a different, profound tiredness, less muscular fatigue than an overwhelming longing to sleep. It is a little like despair. If it were not for glimpsing Iswor waiting above, I might curl up among the rocks and close my eyes. As it is, with suppressed alarm, I wonder for the first time if I will finish this journey.

Suddenly, in bewilderment, I feel the air too thin to sustain me. It is changed, empty. But there is nothing else. I am inhaling in panicky gasps. Nothing remains but this thread of oxygen. It is not enough. Barely enough. Faint, I am lying on stones. The air is receding from me, everything depleted. My breath is rasping sobs.

For long minutes I remain inert as my lungs calm and the fear fades. A memory rises, a pang of sadness, which for a moment I cannot locate. I stand up gingerly and open my mouth to the faint breeze. But the air in my memory is normal. It is her heart that is failing. My own breath stills. Only with consciously deepened inhalations has the shock passed, and the fragile trinity of heart, lungs and blood composed itself.

As she calls out for air, I hook the oxygen mask over her face, and turn on the cylinder. Her hands come up to clasp it, comforted. I can give her twelve minutes, the doctor said, after that it is dangerous. But when I remove the mask, my mother's hands go on clutching it. It is as if I were taking away her life. Later she says: 'Next year I won't be like this. Next year I'll be looking after you.'

In the hospital ward, beyond the curtains closing off the bed, the voices of other patients ring out normal, ugly. A woman upbraids her daughter for visiting her late. Another

74

says she wants to go back to East Grinstead, where her sister can nurse her. A visiting husband recounts a failed burglary at his office. Somebody says: 'I know I'm self-pitying, but I can't help it . . .'

But she hears nothing. Only sometimes her hand clasps mine.

In the ward at night: the wheezing of oxygen, moans and dreams. Winking lights. Who or what is she clasping? Am I still there? The nurses know less than I do. Somebody cries out in another ward.

Morning voices outside our curtains again. I am angry that they will live on.

She lies at last in silence, turned to the window, and her face is young again.

At evening we near the foot of the Torea pass. I hear my breathing with remote amazement. I remember ancient juniper trees along the way, shedding their bark in swathes, like the remains of some long-discarded incarnation. Ram has set up our tents on a plateau above the track. I fall into mine without eating or undressing, and sleep for nine hours.

CHAPTER SIX

· · · · · · ·

In his monastery's garden in Kathmandu, Tashi talked of the retreat from secular life not only as a deliverance from hardship but as the path to a kind of purity. He imagines his native Bhutan to be the heir and guardian of Tibetan Buddhism.

'They say we are like Tibet used to be. In my village the moment you step out of doors you sense people's faith. In the marketplace, on the street. It's not like here in Kathmandu. Here, the moment I'm beyond the monastery gates the beggars come crowding in and people are harassing you to buy things. And so you feel pity. You want to please them, you want to give, but you cannot. In my village there's nothing like that. We were a family of ten, and we were happy. But I haven't been back for four years. When the winter holidays come, only I am missing.'

'Is it so far?'

'Yes, it's far. Once a year I speak to my mother on the phone, just to hear her voice.' He smiled. 'I miss them.'

'Why did you leave?'

'Our lives were very poor. When I saw how my parents worked in the fields, and how they had to take my eldest sister out of school to join them, I knew I didn't want that life. I don't know how much my father had to cheat and lie in order to feed us – eight children. He had a job looking after the company armoury, but would leave it to catch fish whenever he could. He must have caused suffering to many fish, to feed us . . . What do Christians say about things like that?'

I rummaged in my memory. But Jesus's apostles left the lake of Galilee not out of pity for fish, but concern for humans. Tashi's face had an almost contrite gentleness. When I looked at him, I wondered how compassion formed. But he answered that Buddhism was a science, that compassion could be taught, that you could train for it. Just as you could steer yourself away from sex, if you had the will.

I asked: 'Have you never wanted to marry?'

'In the village I have married friends, happy with their children. But it's not for me. Marriage means trouble. I couldn't cope with it.'

He laughed without embarrassment. I could not tell what, if anything, this artless reply concealed, from me or from himself. He folded his robes more closely round his shoulders. 'I was fifteen when I thought: I want to be a monk.'

The poverty from which Tashi fled is printed on all these villages of the high Himalaya, whose idyll is a mirage. Beyond 11,000 feet, erosion gashes half the slopes, and stains them with arteries of drifting scree. My group goes in happy disorder, Ram swinging a can of paraffin, Dhabu clutching the ludicrously awkward stove before him like a totem, Pearl his horse sauntering in front, piled with the tents. In this stripped land I soon see them moving effortlessly a mile or more ahead of us.

We are ascending an empty valley. On either side the snow ranges no longer shine beyond dark-wooded foothills in a dimension of their own, but barge straight down in naked spurs into the abyss where their snowmelt joins the river. As the sun clouds, the air grows cold. Iswor has exchanged his shorts for army fatigues, and is worrying about his hair ('It looks like a yak's coat'). When we cross the 12,000-foot Torea pass, my earlier breathlessness is only a memory. The land is starkly beautiful. The clouds that push from the side valleys hang almost at eye level. The high snows, closing off our passage at either end, reassemble as we walk, sliding aside to reveal mountains higher still. The valley is tightening round us. In the stunted scrub the bird-song thins to plaintive clicks and cheeps, and then to silence.

Into this stillness the traders come swinging round the mountainsides behind their files of mules and horses. We follow their trail for hours – the soles of discarded shoes, excrement, dribbles in the dust (the animals urinate on the move), scraps of faded cloth and broken harness. They are all Bhotias and local Tibetans now, swarthy, wild-faced men whose backs are sheathed in fleeces and yak pelts and foreheads rumpled by headbands to steady their toppling loads. They camp where they can, in caves and abandoned sheep pens. One of them stops dead on the path before me ('He hasn't seen a Westerner before,' says Iswor) and fixes me unbudging with a black, fascinated stare, while his shaggy train of *jhaboo*s – a hybrid of the sleepy Indian cow and the recalcitrant yak – wanders on untended.

On the far side of the river a tortuous and faded trail takes its own way to Tibet westwards above the dwindling Kumuchhiya. It was by this route that Gyato Wangdu, the last Khampa freedom fighter against the Chinese, led his tiny force towards the safety of India. The Khampa warrior tribesmen of eastern Tibet had fought the Chinese occupation ever since 1956, and retreated at last to guerrilla bases over the Nepalese border, nurtured by the CIA. But as the Western rapprochement with China began, the United States withdrew its support, and in July 1974 the Dalai Lama asked the depleted warriors to lay down their arms to the Nepalese army. They did so with proud reluctance. Some of them preferred suicide by drowning or slitting their throats. Only their charismatic leader Wangdu, with a handful of followers, made as if to obey, then rode defiantly away. The Chinese and Nepalese armies hunted him down, and it was by the goat track climbing westwards from where we walked that he opted for a drastic short cut to India and safety. Some twenty miles beyond, and barely five miles from the border, he was ambushed by the Nepalese and fell in a hail of bullets: the last, hopeless spark of his people's armed resistance.

Now at the track's foot the village of Yari is soft with fields of barley and millet. It is a tiny, scattered place where the Bhotia squaws and their ruffianly men, sporting scant turbans, have cleared the earth for crops, piling the excavated rocks alongside, and the valley higher up alternates tilled brown fields with tracts of brilliant green, where wooden conduits bring down water.

After a mile this oasis falls behind. We are approaching

13,000 feet, and a chill wind is blowing fine dust up the valley behind us. Our way snakes across balding scrublands. The track is seared to rubble. Above us the last rivulets drop from the high snows, nudging stones down slopes already cobwebbed with shale. Once we hear goatherds whistling to their flocks far below.

As we go higher, the horizon ahead starts to mesmerise. The snowfields that gleam through the valley cleft resemble an isolated mountain (in fact they are part of a range) and bring a surge of excitement. By the time we pitch our tents under the Nara pass, a heady expectation has set in. For this 15,000-foot defile is our last barrier before Tibet. Now a cold, light rain comes down. I lie in my tent, waiting for it to pass, and imagining the view from the summit of the Nara-la tomorrow. The intimation of change that frontiers bring, a whisper even of revelation, is heightened in this rarefied air by the unearthly aura still shed from Tibet. All myth, I know, should have been wiped from the despoiled country long ago. Yet under this last, formidable pass the afterglow continues of a land breathing an air of its own, and entered through a mystic gap in the mountains and a breach in time. I open my map to see how close we are. The rain clatters like hail on the tent roof. Even on the map's large scale the frontier is only a little finger's breadth away.

This feel of entering a sanctuary has not only moved travellers but has haunted the Tibetans themselves. For centuries they have envisaged a holy land of their own, invisible or inaccessibly remote. The precise location of this kingdom of Shambala is uncertain, but it is said to lie encircled by impassable snow peaks somewhere north of Kailas. Yogis have thought it a three-month journey beyond the mountain, but the path is so elusive that pilgrims find themselves wandering hopelessly. Some even have a notion that Shambala floats in another dimension of time, as if through a galactic wormhole, and can be accessed only by ice doors in the Himalaya. Patterned like an eight-petalled lotus, radiating tributary kingdoms, it has been ruled for two and a half millennia by a dynasty of godly kings who reside in a jewel-built palace, as at the heart of a gorgeous mandala. No word for 'enemy' or 'war' is known here. Its founding king was taught by the Buddha himself, and as his subjects grew more selfless, so their country faded from human sight. Yet its rulers continue to watch over the human world, and after 400 years, as that world falls deeper into ruin, the last redeemer king will ride out from his sanctum to institute a golden age.

In the West, even before the fictional creation of Shangri-La, people toyed with the idea that Shambala geographically existed. The nineteenth-century Hungarian scholar de Körös reckoned he had pinpointed it by astronomic calculation, and in the late 1920s the Russian Nicholas Roerich undertook a long, earnest expedition in constant apprehension of it.

The origins of the myth may lie in the memory of some lost homeland, perhaps the kingdom of Shang-shung around Kailas, subsumed by war in the eighth century. But more likely it entered Tibet from India two and a half centuries later, in the mystical scripture called the Kalacakra Tantra, which details the meditational pathway to Shambala. This teaching, long precious to Tibetan Buddhism, has today accrued a poignant promise. To some, the Chinese ruin of their homeland portends the coming salvation. The Dalai Lama, who believes that a hidden Shambala actually exists, has many times given the Kalacakra initiation in public, gathering souls towards a paradise of several meanings. To those with purified eyes, Shambala exists on earth, while tantric adepts reach its holy land in meditation. But still others imagine it an empire of the future, to be established in the year 2425, when the peace-spreading armies of the last king burst from their mountain cloister.

Meanwhile other sanctuaries pervade the land. The secret entrances to these *beyul*, it is said, were described in buried treasure texts by Padmasambhava, and will be revealed in times of peril. A few *beyul* have already been discovered and settled by expectant communities in the remote Himalaya. To the mundane eye they are no more than tranquil valleys; but to the initiate they shimmer with mystic potential. After the Chinese invasion, it is said, certain lamas led their disciples into the wastelands in search of these *beyul*, following the abstruse directions of sacred texts. Some gave up in despair, but others, it was rumoured, entered cliffs and waterfalls, and vanished beyond human time for ever.

For an hour, as the sun descends, a hard wind blows dust up the valley and into our tents. The rain has lightened. Beneath us the last tributary has drifted and died westwards, and the balding slopes cradle a floor of sudden green called the Sipsip Meadows, strewn with isolated rocks. Snowmelt threads the grass in icy rivulets, while above us the Nara pass is black with cloud. In the dusk I go down towards a massive boulder stranded in the valley. The air is still, purified. The last birdsong has petered out. Only a half-tame finch with white underwings gets up from under my feet, and black butterflies are feeding on the dust.

All day the only plants I have noticed are the worn tapestries of broom over sheltered slopes, and a coral-coloured rock rose flaring alone. Hour after hour a colourless erosion has been setting in. But now, underfoot, spreads a glaze of delicate flowers I do not know, and the ground-hugging shrubs are starred with lemony blooms. It is easy to understand how the first field botanists here – men like Kingdon-Ward and George Sherriff – became obsessed by these brilliant outpourings into the void, and could risk their lives hunting *Primula eburnea* or the blue poppy. It is like spring in the Arctic tundra. Your eyes drop from the empty mountains to this fragile-looking parquetry. White anemones spring up among the brush, and nests of deep pink buds are opening.

It is nightfall when I reach the boulder. It bulges ancient and solitary above the valley. I can descry faint carvings on it, and somebody in these solitudes has picked out in blue chalk the *Om mani padme hum* inscribed on its northern face. But its sculptured Buddhas have almost faded. They float across it on their lotus thrones, their hands cupped or raised or vanished. They must have been carved here to sanctify the pre-Buddhist wilderness – the passes swarm with pagan spirits – but the hands lifted in blessing are barely discernible now, and the haloed heads have withdrawn into the stone.

CHAPTER SEVEN

· · · · · · ·

At first light a herd of goats comes jostling and trampling through our campsite. Their herdsmen are Humla traders in conical caps and buccaneer headscarves, who let out whistling yells as their charges canter between the tents. Every goat carries on its back a little faded saddle-pack filled with salt from Tibet, which will be carried south for ten or fifteen days to be exchanged for grain or rice on the return journey.

This immemorial trade is dying now. Iodised salt from India is selling in the foothills, but a profit can still be made if the herd is as numerous as this one. Its goats are robust but mercurial. No two are alike. Dilapidated white faces peer from tangled black coats, and creamy fleeces charge alongside rufous and skewbald ones. Their horns are magnificently various. Some twirl upwards in barley-sugar spires, lending their owners a rakish and debonair authority; others sweep back as if wind-blown; still others coil demurely against the head, like old-fashioned curls, or droop uselessly downward. But one and all have insolent yellow eyes and devil-may-care tempers, so the stocky sheepdogs run busy alongside, and wherever the goats pass their grazing deepens erosion.

A century ago this traffic was the lifeblood of Humla. Salt and borax from the alkaline Tibetan lakes sold like gold dust on the Nepalese plains, along with the prized Tibetan wool; and the sheep and goat trains returned to Tibet with foodstuffs and the wares of British India: kerosene, soap, matches, even trilby hats. Before the Chinese closed the border in the 1960s, Tibetan tribespeople were a frequent sight on these paths, trading wool for grain. In winter they reached Kathmandu to deal in precious stones, and their communal friendships with Nepalese merchants would be sealed by vows to Kailas and its holy lake.

Chinese regulations have destroyed these old partnerships, or driven them underground, and the goods entering Tibet from China have drastically tilted the trade balance. In exchange for Chinese manufactures – including alcohol – comes the clandestine trade in timber, and now, as the goats flood down the valley in a commotion of dust and bells, a caravan of thirty yaks and *jhaboo*s is heading the other way, shouldering pine logs towards the pass. Beneath the yaks' shaggy petticoats their tread is slow, almost delicate. Their heads stoop, as if overwhelmed by the weight of their massive horns. Their manes jangle with tasselled bells. They are all but immune to the snow that can bury the sheep and goats on these high passes, and the isolated police are either bribed or turn a blind eye to their passage.

We break camp as they go. The tatters of night rain hang about the valley to our east. Clouds like battle-smoke drift against the farther mountains, parting here and there to reveal disembodied crags and ridges. Above us the Nara pass is misted into the sky, and our track thins to a stony path that curves around the shoulder of a mountain we cannot see. We climb by shelves of lichened rock and shale, and hear the last snowmelt trickling alongside. The air feels wrong, as if it holds nothing in it. We are ascending 2,000 feet in less than three hours. For the first time I hear Iswor pant, whereas Ram, who comes from a region near Everest, blithely overtakes us and disappears into the mist. I shorten my steps, inhale deeper. I fear the first throbbing of altitude sickness, but feel nothing. We are approaching the 15,000-foot summit, but my breathless gasping, with its pang of memory, does not return.

An old Bhotia merchant descends towards us with two mules. As he draws near, he lets out a plaintive cry. He needs medicine. Pointing back to the pass where he has come, he touches his chest, coughs and chokes. It is the noise of an old engine trying to start up. Guiltily I hand him aspirin, which cannot palliate him. Iswor says: 'I think no good.' The trouble sounds deep inside the old man's lungs or heart. He stoops his thanks and smiles sadly, hardily. I want to take him in my arms. He drives his mules on, without turning.

The low-clinging cloud has lifted behind us, and suddenly we are walking in sunlight, our shadows sharp underfoot. The mountains stand in thinner, clearer air. All across the horizon now they shine in unearthly clarity, piled on one another in pyramids and flying buttresses of snow. To the north the peaks of the Nalakanka Himal harden in the sunlight, and confront us like a cold amphitheatre on the naked track.

Soundlessly above me, a lammergeyer comes flying out of the pass on motionless wings. The craning of its head shows clear from far below, and its slim, buff body gleams like a brass torpedo between dusky underwings. With no beat of its ten-foot wings, it quarters the slopes below me in leisurely glides, perhaps seeking a thermal on which to rise, then plummets from sight.

We follow its flight path with awe, then turn uphill again. A cold wind hits us as we near the head of the pass, and out of nowhere a light, hard snow is falling. A few minutes later we are lying under a cairn of pallid stones on the summit. It is crowned by bleached tangles of prayer flags. They are strung across the path like old clotheslines, and rasp and stretch in the ice-filled wind. Every traveller who passes tosses another stone on the man-made heap, and sometimes shouts a greeting to the local gods. But we are alone. The snow trickles like blossom over us. The prayer flags are Buddhist, of course, but the spirits of the place are older than faith, and spiteful. The *nyen* live on mountaintops close to the sky. The cairns are their altars. They unleash blizzards and avalanches, brew up blinding mists. It is wise to offer them a stone. More trouble still are the *tsen*, who materialise out of thin air. They were said to be powerful in the days of Shang-shung kings, around Kailas, and they ride red-skinned and armoured through the mountains, shooting plague-tipped arrows. Iswor offers them a second stone, and we lie back at peace under the falling snow.

It is not hard to see in these spirits a memory of Tibetan raiders, who centuries ago descended the passes in chain mail, their faces daubed with ochre. Such traces of a militant people defy the later image of a remote and otherworldly theocracy, but the country's early history suggests a people in love with war. In the seventh and eighth centuries, when the Tang dynasty reached its height, the Tibetan armies with their Turkish auxiliaries marched through the Chinese empire and sacked the capital, Changan, a thousand miles to the east. For generations Tibet stood on a war footing, and its armour was the finest in the world. The Chinese wrote in awe that impenetrable chain mail sheathed the elite spearmen – even horses – from head to toe, and that in battle they never retreated, but a new rank of soldiers moved implacably into the place of the fallen. They could field 200,000 men at a time, it was said, and despised a tranquil death. For two centuries they dominated the southern Silk Road oases, reaching even Samarkand, so that the Arab caliph Haroun-al-Rashid sought alliance with the Chinese against them. Southwards they thrust beyond Nepal and crossed the Indian plain to invade Burma.

Even after Buddhism filled the land with monasteries, the monks protected their faith with arms. Alongside lives of prayer and meditation, the fourteenth and fifteenth centuries were rife with monastic civil war, sometimes waged in league with Mongol chiefs, and the Dalai Lamas (if they were not murdered in childhood) were complicit in violence even into the early twentieth century. Travellers often noted in the Tibetan men an earthy emotionalism, quick to draw a dagger, and into the mid-century dacoits and predatory nomads, armed with matchlocks and Russian revolvers, were the plague of pilgrims.

A few paces over the Nara-la, the snow is thinning away. As we crest the pass, an enormous mountain barrier rises to meet us. Nothing sounds but the wind in our ears, even the purling of snow water gone. Here, where the Nepalese Himalaya drop in giant steps to the plateaux of Tibet, the last mountain walls, slashed by gullies, climb vertiginously north toward Kailas and the peaks beyond, lit by the gleam of glaciers in mid-air, and ridges hollowed with unmelting snow.

Under these obliterating skylines we descend a widening valley, where the Karnali, re-emerging from impassable gorges, cuts a corridor at last into sunlight. Between one step and another a stark change comes down. Centuries of monsoons have exhausted themselves over the heights behind us, and on this bitter counterscarp only blackened scrub survives. Precipitously beneath us the last grey-pink ravines of Nepal plunge to the Karnali, then level out towards another country. All becomes light and sky. Far to our north-west there opens up a land of planetary strangeness, empty of life, under a void of brilliant blue. We are gazing at a tableland that was once the Tethys Sea. Forty-five million years ago, as the tectonic plate of India – then a separate continent – crashed into the underbelly of Asia, and the Himalaya erupted to the south, this primordial ocean drained away. Marine fossils still exist in the Tibetan plateau, betraying that the highest country in the world was once an ocean.

As we struggle down the fault line of this momentous convulsion, a new vista eases open. In this rarefied air, where a person may be distinctly descried ten miles off, I glimpse with a catch of the heart the violet-tinged steppes of Tibet shelving north-west. Beyond them, an unbroken line of mountains glimmers across the horizon under cauliflower clouds that look as static as they are; while in the distant north floats the 25,000-foot Gurla Mandhata, which shines above the holy lake of Manasarovar. In its vivid stillness the land might be a painted backdrop slotted into the valley cleft beyond us. The artist wanted to express an inhuman tranquillity, and thought up this.

The country is fearsomely alone. The same geologic clash that created the Tibetan plateau circled it with the mountains that protect and desiccate it: the Karakoram in the west, the desert-swept Kunlun to the north. Even in the more vulnerable east, hundreds of miles of near-empty upland divide Tibet from the nearest easy habitat. Of its few million inhabitants, most are crowded into the more fertile valleys of the south-east. Compared to these, the far west, where we are going, is still more pitilessly dry and cold. In this thinned air, three miles above sea level, drastic temperature changes crack boulders and pulverise cliffs. The sun's radiation is so intense that its heat surges from the earth to draw in icy winds and dust storms that sandpaper the land smooth. In a single day snowfall may alternate with thunder, hail and blistering sun.

We clamber down towards the frontier by slopes already fractured and slippery. Torrents of shale oversweep the track. The colours around us are pastel grey and shell pink. Whole valley sides are a confusion of debris sliding between shields of darker rock. Their spurs bulge like flayed bones. Sometimes our way is littered with igneous boulders that glint like beetles' wings, and once we trudge across virgin snow.

The Karnali winds green beneath us, flowing fast from the gorges where we have not followed it. Take a careless step and you could slide unstoppably 200 feet or more into its ravine. We reach it at last down knee-jarring rocks and gravel, and a few minutes later we are walking into the frontier settlement of Hilsa.

Ten years ago, Iswor says, Hilsa was no more than a huddle of cottages and tents. Now it drifts along the river in a sordid trickle of blue-grey stone, half-built or deserted dwellings, and its tottering wooden gangplank has been replaced by a clanking cable suspension bridge, hung with prayer flags and washing. Cascades of rubbish pour beneath it into the river: Chinese beer bottles and layers-deep plastic. The Tibetan frontier is on the far side, a few hundred yards away. A Chinese road is being stretched down close to the Karnali to the grumble of bulldozers. The traders' caravans cross the bridge with bovine ease, the yaks and *jhaboo*s indifferent to the thin treads under their hooves and to the river boiling fifty feet below. Flagrantly they carry their contraband timber to the trading post of Sher over the low hill beyond, where they exchange it at knockdown prices for clothes, flour and drink. On our side the police post is busy dealing in alcohol.

We find a hostel for Nepalese merchants. Its dirt-floored rooms are disintegrating around a courtyard piled with yak dung for winter fuel. Our beds are planks propped against the walls. Wooden saddles and rotting harness lie stacked under them. Whenever we doze, the smeared windows darken with the faces of children peering fascinated in. This Thakuri family has moved from poverty downriver, bringing their estate with them – three ponies and a cow – hoping to prosper here. But they have only found poverty again. They are listless and shy. The

Colin Thubron

father wears an England football vest, made in China. He hopes to attract trekkers. And he dreams of merchants bedding down while their beasts slumber in the dung-filled courtyard, as in some Arab caravanserai. But there is nobody but us, and his children playing in the dust.

We sit in their room at evening with a group of silent neighbours, while his wife brews tea and suckles a weak baby under her pullover. Sometimes, the man says, they are allowed to take a sick child to the Tibetan clinic over the river. They have crossed the border often, to trade something in Taklakot. But on this side there is no clinic, no school. 'We wait for things to get better. The Maoists are gone now. They are in Kathmandu.' They glance uncertainly at one another. 'We have never been to Kathmandu.'

Soon afterwards the flue from their stove, which zigzags in rusty segments to the roof, turns red hot and sparks the timber ceiling into flames. The men gaze at it unmoving, as if at their fate, while the woman plucks the baby from her breast and scrambles on to the roof with a jug of water.

Their depression starts to affect us. We hand out medicine for their chest coughs and headaches – they accept it without a word – then trail away to sleep. Iswor does not trust this place, and Ram jams the door shut with trekking poles. For a long time I lie on the plank bed, unsleeping. The light of a gibbous moon trickles through the grimed window and on to the mud floor. I watch it moving like a promise. In a week's time this moon will have filled out to mark the Buddhist holy month of Saga Dawa, and pilgrims will be gathering under Mount Kailas.

CHAPTER EIGHT

· · · · · · ·

In the restless night – the village dogs howling from the
rubbish heaps – I have a dream whose memory fades on
waking, leaving an aftermath of celebration, so that I try
to re-enter it but can barely retrieve its last, faltering
images. In the blackness of the room a sliver of dawn opens
from the doorway. Dhabu the horse drover is going home.
We crawl like caterpillars from our sleeping bags, and
Ram cooks up a breakfast of chapati and eggs. Dhabu
receives his wages with cupped hands, and is bright
with thoughts of his village. This is in the mountains by
Dharapuri, a few miles short of Simikot, and he will reach
it in three days on a journey that has taken us a week. In
his shy response to my farewell (in Iswor's lapidary trans-
lation) he is already homesick.

'My parents are there, and my wife. I want to get back to
her, to see her again. She is my friend.' He nibbles at his
chapati, as if he should not be with us.

'And your children?'

'I have four. Two died.'

I ask: 'How was that?'

'I don't know. One was five, another seven. I don't know
why.'

Iswor says gently: 'He has no education, you see.'

'The nearest clinic is over the mountains, many miles away,' Dhabu says. He looks less sad than bemused, as if at some inexplicable order. 'My village is poor, peaceful. We own one field, which is not enough. So I work like this, with my horse Moti-moti . . .'

I wonder aloud how long he can sustain it.

'I will finish when the journey of my life is over, that is when I will end.'

I touch his hand, wondering how many peoples conceive life as a journey, time as a road.

But he says: 'I am happy. My life is good.'

I say laughing: 'You have a happy face.' It is long and humorous (although he does not smile), framed in bats' ears and a tent of rumpled hair.

He touches his features, as if confirming them. 'Good.'

I watch him depart, with Moti following. He turns back once and, from this distance, dares to lift his hand and smile. Iswor beside me says: 'That is a very simple man.'

Now that the horse is gone, we must use Tibetan transport on the far side to carry us to Taklakot, the region's traditional trading centre, and on to Kailas. But we cannot cross the frontier alone. Chinese suspicion brands the lone traveller here as maverick or spy. His solitude is otherwise inexplicable. Without a group he is too elusive, slips beyond control. But somewhere behind us marches the party of seven British trekkers under whose camouflage I hope to cross. They should be here by evening. Iswor carries a satellite phone by which he might have reached them, but he never turns it on.

We leave the hostel without regret, pitch our tents in rough ground among ruins in Hilsa's outskirts, and wait. The prospect of the trekkers touches me with foreboding. These past days I have felt a stressless self-diffusion, as if my own culture were growing lighter on my shoulders. I will not welcome its return in others. I have too much imagined these mountains as mine.

Iswor and I wander the derelict settlement alone. Only a few barley fields surround its no-man's-land, and every other structure is half-built or falling down. A desultory wind whips up the dust. The inhabitants all seem transient, here to exploit the border trade. No one was born in Hilsa. Yet the place is built on a sediment of Chinese waste: Pepsi-Cola cans and split trainers, cigarette cartons, Lhasa beer bottles, old tins of engine oil. Women and children digging foundations burrow among stones and trash together. Everyone is swathed anonymous against the dust. But for the first time in days I set eyes on a wheeled machine: a little Chinese tractor that must have driven over the bridge or through the water. There is even a wonky wheelbarrow.

We stop beside the bridge. On the far side stands the clean stem of a Chinese electricity pylon – there is no electricity in Hilsa – and we hear the growl of earth-moving where the tarmac road is descending to the river. Iswor says quaintly: 'I am sad for looking.'

'What is it?'

'The Chinese . . . We do not have their future. We are not a developing people like them.' He keeps his back turned on Hilsa, frowning, as if its hovels parodied his life.

'Perhaps this place is forgot by us. Kathmandu is far from here. Even Simikot is far.'

Weeks later, when I visited Iswor's village birthplace high in the hills above Kathmandu valley, I understood a little. Circled by far mountains, its terraced maize and vegetables, cherry and peach trees touched it with an illusion of self-sufficiency. A small Hindu temple and a Buddhist stupa rested side by side. Doors and lintels showed old carving, and dark overlapping roof tiles turned the houses to ancient and precious reptiles nesting in the orchards.

Iswor's parents had migrated to Kathmandu in his child-hood, but returned to the village for leisure and to manage their few fields. But his eldest brother Bishu was a celebrity. Iswor languished in his shadow. Bishu had climbed Everest with an Indian army team, and was dubbed a 'summiteer'. His job in a Kathmandu travel agency was well-paid, and he owned two houses and some land. When he visited from the city, the young men's hands clasped together in hero-worship, and the old hurried to greet him. Walking one day in the June-scented pine woods above the village, he told me: 'Iswor's job is not so frequent, not so rich. I don't know what will happen to him. Maybe he will come back here and do farming . . .'

But Iswor didn't want to farm. He wanted to succeed in the cruel labyrinth of Kathmandu. 'The young are bored in the village,' he said. 'It's only two hours by motorbike from the city, so they go in and get jobs as clerks, drivers, any-thing.'

'And what happens to the villages?'

He said what I already know: that they become the ghetto of the unenterprising, the sick, the old. It was the same all over Asia. Sometimes the villages were sustained by women. Often they fell to absentee landlords. On their picturesque hillsides they started to go silent.

But you would not have guessed this that night. The young men danced and sang on a hillside by the blaze of a log fire: old Hindu songs, Iswor said, which they had learnt in childhood. A man with Down's syndrome – his Mongoloid features subsumed among the Tamang faces round him – gyrated alone in his dirty smock, frenzied by the music. Far into the night the youths went on singing and tapping their *damphu* drums, and if an invisible divide existed between those who had returned from the city on holiday and those who had greeted them, it was blurred by allegiances deeper than success, and by the old remembered music under the village stars.

The women kept away or watched shyly from the dark. The older wore bright saris. But no, Iswor said, he could not marry one, and repeated his refrain: 'They have no education.'

Only one girl gentled his voice when he spoke of her: his thirteen-year-old youngest sister, back in Kathmandu. 'I love her. I want to help her continue at school, even if my parents don't afford it. Her oldest sister will leave the home soon, and then she will be alone.' He grimaced into the dying firelight. Just as he was to Bishu, perhaps, so the small girl was to her elder sister. He spoke as if she were an orphan, or a shadowy afterthought. 'She will be very sad . . .'

His poverty seemed only to exacerbate this brotherly

dream. She alone, it appeared, had touched his complicated heart.

The seven British trekkers trickle in at evening, and pitch their tents by ours. They are not the hearty group I had feared, but middle-aged and quiet. They have come for scenic beauty and physical challenge. Most are experienced trekkers. Their leader prefers his groups older, he says. Often the young are less fit, and do not know their limits. Our transient union brings luxuries. We eat in a dining tent on rickety camp chairs. From time to time the wind rattles its poles loose and collapses some canvas on to us. Nobody complains or expects much. We feast on dumplings and omelettes, and morning porridge. Their sherpas rig up a modest lavatory tent above an excavated hole.

At evening, as I linger with Iswor by the Hilsa bridge, where the Karnali now flows brown with dust, the goat and sheep herds come barging and bullying across it, aborting all human traffic, until a column of yaks displaces them and I cross for a moment into Tibet. On this bank, beneath a sagging barbed-wire fence, a low plinth is carved *China* in Chinese characters on its far side, *Nepal* in Nepali on the other. But the flimsy gate is closed. I sit down on the plinth – one leg in Nepal, the other in Tibet – and gaze where we will go, with luck, tomorrow.

But few Western travellers entered by this secretive Karnali. They came by more accessible passes from India in the west. The first European to set eyes on Mount Kailas, the Jesuit missionary Ippolito Desideri, in 1715, had toiled there from Ladakh, sometimes snow-blind and coughing blood.

Had he and his companion not fallen in with the caravan of a Tartar princess travelling to Lhasa, they would probably have died. Some six weeks later, in consternation, Desideri passed beneath a bitterly cold and cloud-wrapped Kailas. For days on end, he wrote, pilgrims circled the foot of this dread peak, whose sanctity was deepened by a certain Urghien (Padmasambhava), the founder of their religion. Here, centuries ago, the saint had meditated in a cave now celebrated by a few monks in a wretched monastery.

For five astonishing years Desideri, a man of keen learning, preached among the Tibetans in mutual tolerance and curiosity. But in 1721 he was recalled to the Vatican. Bigotry and turmoil ensued, with Mongol invasion, and in 1745 the last missionaries were expelled from Tibet. As the years went on, the country's borders became encrusted with hopeful Christian outposts, longing to enter. When the land fell to Christ, some believed, the Last Day would dawn. But the Tibetans never allowed missions into the heart of their country again.

For a century after Desideri, no known European set eyes on Kailas. Then in 1812 the erratically brilliant veterinary surgeon William Moorcroft, with his shady companion Hyder Hearsey, made their way here disguised as Hindu ascetics. Moorcroft, intent equally on exploration and pioneering commerce, purchased a herd of fifty pashmina goats to drive back into India, and combed the Manasarovar lake to discover if any of India's great rivers had its source there. Three years later he vanished into Central Asia, where his papers turned up piecemeal long afterwards, fomenting the mystery around his death.

The source of the great rivers – the Ganges, Brahma-putra, Indus and Sutlej – became an obsession in London and British India, and remained uncertain even into the early twentieth century. As if by divine intent, all four of them rose close to Mount Kailas, echoing 2,000-year-old Hindu scriptures. Yet by the mid-nineteenth century Tibet was being breached not by explorers but by army officers and civil servants on big-game hunting forays. Defying the ban by both British and Tibetan authorities, they slipped over the Zanskar passes with their servants. On these illicit journeys the magnificent and controversial topography they were treading went largely unrecorded. They were more concerned with potting an *Ovis ammon* or a wild yak, and they treated Tibetan law with cavalier disdain. One Scottish aristocrat even sailed a rubber dinghy on the sacred waters of Manasarovar, for which the local governor was beheaded.

Yet Tibetan officials were often quaintly peaceful in their efforts to repel these foreigners. They complained that they themselves would be executed if they failed. One traveller reported a whole troop of soldiers who fell pathetically on their faces, drawing their hands across their throats in sign of their own fate. Even the bigoted Henry Savage Landor (grandson of the vile-tempered poet), who wrote a gaudy account of his ordeal, was only physically assaulted after every other measure to turn him back had failed.

The true survey of Tibet at this time was achieved by Indian pandits, trained by the British and disguised as merchants or holy men. Their piously fingered rosaries were in fact recording distances, and their prayer wheels were stuffed with coded data. Even after the brutal British invasion of Tibet under Younghusband in 1904, travel for foreigners was no easier. In 1907 the Swedish explorer Sven Hedin — a man of self-blinding vision — had to enter by subterfuge. He then spent fifteen months following a thousand-mile broken arc of mountains eastwards across inner Tibet, and became the first European to reach the source of the Indus — and to join the pilgrims circling Kailas.

Humbler travellers, of course, had been entering the country for centuries: pilgrims who left no record. In a land of bitter extremes, racked by armed dacoits riding hardy ponies and yaks, they were wretchedly vulnerable, protected only by their poverty. Some of the brigands were themselves on pilgrimage. Others routinely contributed a share of their plunder to the monasteries. The fastidious Japanese monk Ekai Kawaguchi, while circling Kailas, noticed a notorious bandit and murderer praying to the mountain in penance not only for his past crimes, but for those he expected to commit in the future.

Kawaguchi himself was one of the first and most perceptive pilgrims to recount his journey, in 1900. He was perhaps a spy; yet fervently pious. After surviving early vicissitudes (including a nomad girl's assault on his virginity), he prostrated himself a ritual 108 times on the first sight of Kailas, then broke into poetry and circled the holy mountain for four days in ecstasy.

But it was Hindu pilgrims who penned the most ardent journeys. Eighteen years after Kawaguchi, the swami Bhagwan Hamsa, a girlishly fragile figure, found his own salvation on Kailas. He too, in high-flown prose, survived countless perils on the way: cobras, ghosts, a lust-crazed elephant, licentious mountain women. On Kailas he stumbled into the glacial cave of a yogi, with whom he spent three days, drinking only water, his head resting in the yogi's lap at night; and beside the frozen lake beyond the highest pass he received a vision of his personal, tantric saint, in whose presence he felt himself diffusing mystically away. The account of his journey later featured an enthusiastic preface by W.B.Yeats, whose poem *Meru* described a world mountain where hermits, 'caverned in night under the drifted snow', might pass finally beyond illusion.

Tibet was still so little known that travellers could imagine it the haven of once-universal mysteries. Echoes of ancient Egypt were divined (some scholars still play with this idea), and the country was even rumoured the fountainhead of the Aryan people, so that Hitler's propagandists took a sentimental look at it. Tibet's present state might be wretched, but its past could be purified. Even the early Christian missionaries entertained fantasies, imagining themselves among a people of lapsed Christianity. The Dalai Lama, after all, enjoyed the veneration and infallibility of a pope (and was likewise mired in politics), protected not by the Holy Roman Emperor but by the Celestial Emperor of China. There were trinities of Buddhist deities. Tara, the goddess of compassion, recalled the Virgin. Protestant intellectuals later castigated Catholics and Buddhists together as idol-worshipping and relic-venerating, alike in their celibate monks, their ritual incense, sprinkled water and rosaries. Strangest of all, as if in mockery of the Eucharist, the oldest Tibetan sects – the

Bon and the Nyingma – preserved a 'life-consecration rite' in which the priest passes a communal bowl of beer and flour pellets among the congregation.

This, perhaps, is a relic of the Nestorian Christianity that had penetrated deep into Central Asia by the sixth century. A thousand years later, Indian sadhus were returning from the north with unverifiable reports that Christian communities lived around Lake Manasarovar, and sparked hopes that somewhere deep in Asia the legendary kingdom of the Christian emperor Prester John survived.

Towards nightfall an old man falters across the Hilsa bridge. With fearful care a young monk, his son, guides his uncertain steps, enfolding his shoulders in one arm, clasping his elbow in the other, as he shepherds him over to Nepal. The bridge rasps and sways. The old man is grimly dignified, dressed in a jacket of embroidered Chinese silk with sheepskin trimmings. His gaze is set on the farther bank, where they find haven in a little walled rest house with rickety balconies.

Later a crowd gathers to stare up at the ridge to the south. Faintly I descry two wavering lines of *bharal*, the rare blue mountain sheep. In the gloom I make out the shifting of their black-stockinged legs against the pale rock, and their backswept horns. Momentarily the young monk comes out too, to see what is happening. He speaks hesitant English. He escaped Tibet to India, he says, and is studying at Dehra Dun. He can never go back – he plucks his orange robes as explanation – but every year his father crosses the border into Humla for four days, and they meet in this no-man's-land, before parting again. Each year he wonders if the crossing of the bridge will be their last.

I remembered another monk I had met that spring. His monastery belonged to the Gelugpa, the sect of the Dalai Lama, and its terraced gardens flowed vivid above the Kathmandu valley. He was slight and pale. I might have been walking beside a ghost. Cuckoos were sounding in the valley beneath us, but the Kathmandu suburbs were already lapping at the hill's foot, and the murmur of road-building rose from the mists. The monk was young, like the monk of Hilsa, and he too had been severed from his past by the Chinese frontier.

He said: 'My family came to Lhasa from our village in Tibet eleven years ago. My father had saved up some Chinese money. We were walking, without papers. I was ten years old. In Lhasa my father and mother gave me over to six others. Then they went back, and I never saw them again. Our group travelled over the plains secretly. Sometimes, I remember, I walked. It grew very hard. Sometimes somebody carried me on his shoulders. It was bitter cold, November. We walked for one month and ten days. I cannot remember how we slept. No relatives came with me. I have none here. Here I left them all behind and became a monk.'

'You wouldn't go back?'

'If I did, the Chinese would take me. I've demonstrated outside the Chinese embassy in Kathmandu, and they photograph you. They must have my face on their files, many times. On the border they recognise us by our Tibetan names.' A gentle rain was falling, but he did not notice. 'My mother is fifty-four now, my father dead. I have two sisters there. The youngest I can't remember. But I have spoken to my mother on the phone.'

'That's something.' But I thought: she will just be a voice to him until she dies. Had his parents, I wondered, been too poor to keep their late-born son, or had they purposely released him into freedom?

He only said: 'I don't know.' Behind us novice monks were running out of their classrooms, shouting and tussling together. 'My family is this monastery now. This is my place. My father, my mother, my brothers, they are all here.'

CHAPTER NINE

· · · · · · ·

I wake to the foraging of mules in the nearby rubbish, where they seem to be munching cardboard, and to a Nepalese police helicopter that lands beside the river in a spiral of dust. Etiquette demands that Nepalese porters carry our baggage across the bridge, and that Tibetan porters relieve them on the far side. The muddy water roars between. The straggling barbed-wire frontier is being breached by bands of goats that scramble over and squeeze through it. As we step through the open gate into Tibet, the sun is hot in a cloudless sky. No official is in sight. We sit on piles of rocks outside two tents for monitoring swine flu, and wait.

As the hours drag by, my expectation starts to wane. Only the anticipation of change has tempered the squalid rootlessness of Hilsa, but this is now seeping away. The sun scorches down. Beside us the Karnali runs dark with the blown dust of the night. I start to fear that the border is closing, as suddenly as it did last year during the riots before the Beijing Olympics. The jittery fiftieth anniversary of the Dalai Lama's flight has only just passed.

By noon there is still no sight of police or medical orderlies. Then we hear that an Indian pilgrim has died on Kailas.

They are bringing his body down. Sobered, we go on waiting. An Indian woman, arrived by helicopter the day
before, sits with us on the rocks, her breast heaving. She has
been to Kailas five times, she says, but her lungs are weak
and she cannot climb much more. This last time she has
brought her ex-husband with her: a silent man retracted
behind dark glasses and a greying mass of beard. I sense she
wants to teach him something.

A squad of porters trudges into sight, bearing the corpse
on an old army stretcher. Three Indian elders walk alongside, but no one seems moved. The man, apparently, died
alone. Other porters spread out one of the plastic canvases
the Chinese use for baggage, and spray it with disinfectant,
while a group of Tibetan women squat nearby, arranging
each other's hair. Casually the body is tipped on to the
canvas, the face covered by a brown cloth. A plump hand
dangles loose, its wrist circled by a golden watch. One of the
Indians produces a roll of sticking-tape and the porters
entwine the corpse until it is half sitting up, while a gang of
road workers lumber to and fro and the Tibetan girls go on
primping their hair. Then the body is carried away across
the bridge.

The Indian woman says sourly that this happens often.
Her government runs small tour groups whose members
are chosen by lottery. They enter Tibet through the northern province of Uttarakhand, acclimatising slowly, and are
medically checked for fitness. Many are refused.

'But the private tour agents are different,' she says. 'They
often make no medical checks at all. They'll enrol anyone.
They just want the money.' Her gaze moves bitterly to the

far bank, where the cortège is stumbling towards the helicopter. 'The people who sign up don't know how hard it will be. Kailas is holy to Lord Shiva, and many pilgrims are Shaivites from the south, from lowland cities like Bangalore and Mumbai. They've never climbed anything except their own stairs. Sometimes they're old.' She glances towards her ex-husband, who looks angry. 'We've come up too fast ourselves – twelve thousand feet in a few hours.'

Three medical orderlies with police and immigration officers arrive together. They are all Chinese, and scrupulously polite. We are lined up outside their tent, exhausted by the sun – I stand with the trekking group – and called in one by one to fill out quaint health questionnaires. *Are you carrying live animal other than dog and cat? ... Have you had close connection with pig during one week? ...* They take our temperatures from thermometers thrust under our armpits. Their smiles are clipped. Perhaps the rough warmth of native life around them has steeled this prim correctitude. They are part of China's gift to Tibet, after all: health, education, infrastructure. They are uniting the motherland. In these life-threatening heights they work among an ungrateful people. Before they came, they've been told, the country was a sink of feudal serfs, with a life expectation of thirty-six, and its people are still insanitary, drunk, illiterate. They surely need to be taught. The orderlies have smart black briefcases, where the data on our health is filed away.

The police too are reticent, even as they empty our backpacks. Their olive uniforms and crimson shoulder flashes look chaste and vaguely unnerving in the surrounding squalor. As the detritus of the past days is spilled out ignominiously on to a bench — old socks, notes, medicine, thermal underwear, trinkets for children — I grow anxious for my densely scribbled diary. A rosy-cheeked captain goes through item by item wearing surgical gloves. But he can barely read English, let alone the ant-like trickle of my handwriting. Only the pamphlet from a Buddhist monastery arrests him, with its photographs of monks. He is hunting for pictures of the Dalai Lama, whose face spreads paranoia along the whole frontier. His fingers fidget along the leaflet's portraits of old, smiling faces: Lama Zopa Rinpoche . . . Lama Lhundrup . . . Once he consults with another officer, and together they scrutinise the picture of an altar where a tiny snapshot is propped. Photo of a photo, can it be he? Impossible to be sure. It's merely a smile under a pair of spectacles.

A wolf in monks' clothing, the Chinese call him. But to Tibetans he is the incarnation of Avalokitesvara, the bodhisattva of compassion. His religious devotions occupy four hours of his day. Yet he rejects the mystification of his person and his image as the spirit of Tibet. He is a man, and transient. His apostleship of peace has brought his country a refracted holiness, but no Chinese concession. The West fetes and wonders at him. As for China, his distrust of material institutions, even of his own office, renders him all but incomprehensible.

But the leaflet of smiling monks is at last returned to me, and an hour later we reach the waiting Land Cruisers, where a Tibetan guide drapes us with the white scarves of his people's welcome, and we start up the half-metalled road towards Taklakot. Behind us the ebbing waves of the

Himalaya hang the sky with spires, while ahead the land smoothes into an ancient silence. In this thinned air everything inessential has been burnt away. We are crossing a wind-scorched tableland under a vacant sky. Its treeless hills roll caramel brown to the horizon. No one else is on the road. We pass two police posts and a ruined fort, and traverse some depleted tributaries of the Karnali. The ochre walls of the Khojarnath monastery fade behind us. Since last year's pre-Olympics riots, the Chinese distrust of monks has deepened, and we are forbidden to enter.

Fifteen miles later we are driving into Taklakot. I look out in bafflement on wide, half-empty streets. They are almost silent. This is Tibet, I tell myself, I am in Tibet. But the town has a lunar placelessness. A millennium ago it was the capital of an independent Tibetan kingdom, and in time its soft cliff caves were home to monks and merchants. It became the crossroads of Indian pilgrims and Nepalese traders bargaining rice, palm sugar and half the artefacts of the lowlands; of the local Drokpa Tibetans exchanging their immemorial wool and salt; of Khampa nomads selling brick tea.

But now the town has the gutted feel of other Chinese frontier places. In the modern district — a cross-hatch of arid avenues — the vanguard of a new civilisation is dourly in place: China Post, the Agricultural Bank of China, China Mobile. Here the Tibetan shops, with their whitewashed façades and roof lines of compacted twigs, go side by side with Chinese restaurants and hair salons, but none seems to be doing business. Their cavernous interiors are barely lit, and several look abandoned. Soldiers in fatigues and plimsolls are waiting outside the Li Fei nightclub – for this is a garrison town – and police cars are nosing out of the lanes.

We arrive at a sterile compound where travellers are insulated in dormitories and stark bedrooms. Its gates are plastered with warnings against swine flu. We might have slipped back to the time before Deng Xiaoping, when foreigners and Chinese – let alone Tibetans – were segregated. Our baggage is emptied again, and our permits in this sensitive area are scrutinised once more by the military. They have grown more nervous, more oppressive, since the riots last year.

I walk out into the chill of evening. Somewhere beyond these streets, above the unseen river, the ancient market district spreads under cliffs, and I grope there by compass, losing myself in the dead ends of alleys, crumbling walls, concrete barracks. At last a few willow trees clear a view. Below me drops the ravine of the Karnali, where the putty-soft cliffs, jagged and split by meltwater, are riddled with caves that are still inhabited. At their feet the white stucco of Tibetan houses, sliced by tapering doors and high, barred windows, appears magically complete. I cross light-hearted over the suspension bridge and wait for the bazaars – hectic with Indian, Humla and Tibetan interchange, trussed clouds of wool, hillocks of rock salt – to break furiously around me.

But I enter a ghost town. A few doorways are still gay with murals, but most stand derelict, their rooms gutted beyond, their windows blocked, the tin pelmets swinging broken from their lintels. As I ascend the street past range after range of these phantom shops, a cold wind gets up from the west. Scarcely a soul is about. Here and there, as in some surreal dream, a rotted billiards table stands upended in the dust.

I ask a group of Tibetan women what has happened, but their Mandarin is worse than mine. The summer market has not worked for two years, they say, banned by the Chinese. They gesture back at the district behind me. Everything has been transferred to the modern zone. They smile in resignation.

A mani wall, the height of a man, wavers to the street's end. Thousands of inscribed stones, the colour of dull rose, are laid one upon another, topped by rose-painted yak skulls. The wall protects nothing, of course, and keeps out no one. It is an act of mass devotion, to be circled praying (although it is deserted) and its immured prayer wheels piously spun.

Beyond it the white walls of Tsegu Gompa, 'the Nine-Storeyed Monastery', emerge from a cliffside pocked with windows and gaping doorways. Galleries beetle over the scarp on sagging piers, but their stairways are cut deep inside the cliff, so that the ochre-splashed balconies disappear and re-emerge across the rock face as in a dilapidated palace.

I climb shivering through the courtyard gates, and call up to no one I can see. Only a ceremonial pole rises from the court. After a long time a shaven head peers down from above, then withdraws. I shout up that I'd like to enter, but nothing happens. I wait bleakly in the dying light. I wonder: will all monasteries exclude me like this? On the balconies the prayer wheel bells tinkle faintly in the wind. Cautiously the head reappears, vanishes again. Then a door opens in the cliff. The monk looks young and frightened. He speaks nothing I understand. He leads me by other doors along a passage sliced into the scarp, then steeply upwards through a cave by an iron ladder in near darkness. One after another, I am groping through a series of airless sanctuaries whose ceilings lour black with lamp smoke, their crevices stuck with Chinese bank notes. In the dimness the walls drip with sacred banners, many faded and rotting, and behind them, perhaps precious in these thirteenth-century shrines, the wall paintings lie so obscure under grime that I can make out nothing.

In the central chapel the benches for praying monks, with the abbot's throne, are toy-like replicas of those in grander monasteries. But the young monk has grown nervously proud. He names the statues to me – although most, in the version he gives, I do not know. They sit in cracked plaster, their blue and orange bodies clouded in yellow scarves. In this darkness they inhabit only pools of chance light, disclosing faces of gaudy indifference: cheap jewellery, bulging eyes, anemone lips. Sometimes a crowd of lamps trembles beneath an altar, although only the monk nurtures them. Here he points out the Sakyamuni Buddha, and here Padmasambhava, whose dead-white face trickles a black moustache, and whose androgynous consort flanks him in painted gold.

It is dusk as I cross back over the river to the compound to sleep. Behind me the riddled cliff face rises black above the valley, while far beyond it the once-great monastery of Shepeling lifts in ruins under the wakening stars. Sixty years ago this powerful hermitage sprawled along the ridge beside the fortress of the district governor, the 'Lord of Purang'. It housed some 170 monks, a school for novices, a vast library and 400 precious banner paintings. In 1967, during the Cultural Revolution, Chinese army artillery levelled it to dust, leaving only the roofless slivers and stubs dissolving into the night above me. A few monks, I later heard, had crept back to the ruins, but this desecrated skyline still loomed unrepented in the dark, like a warning to the div-ided town below.

In a land maimed since 1950 by Chinese occupation, by mass killings and displacement, the Cultural Revolution, with its wholesale destruction of all things old, struck at Tibet's heart. Amid the executions and 'struggle' sessions, all public vestiges of Buddhism were erased, the Buddha denounced as a reactionary, sacred images tossed into latrines, and scriptures converted into shoes for disgraced monks. By 1976, out of more than 6,000 monasteries and temples, thirteen remained.

How much material wealth must Beijing pour into the country before it can dream of seducing this profound Buddhist identity? Where Tibetans sense spirit, the Chinese see superstition. When the Chinese demolished Shepeling monastery, they say, with its treasured scriptures and sixty-foot silken banners, they swept away the remnants of feudal sorcery, together with the skull from which the chief lama drank, and the enshrined testicle of an idolised warrior.

CHAPTER TEN

....

A steep road takes our Land Cruisers north. Behind us the Great Himalaya cover the skyline, while ahead opens an orange and sulphur-coloured wilderness where the Karnali withers away. The 25,000-foot massif of Gurla Mandhata, detached from the Himalaya in its own bright climate, comes shouldering down from the east, and my Tibetan driver, whose dashboard swings with the protective photos of lamas, starts softly to sing.

Near the village of Toyo to our west the most formidable nineteenth-century invader of Tibet came to grief. The Indian general Zorawar Singh, marching in the service of a lightly federated Sikh empire, had already conquered Ladakh and Baltistan, establishing one of the borders of modern India, and in spring 1841 he advanced out of Kashmir with some 500 men, seizing forts as he went. Near Taklakot he routed an 8,000-strong Tibetan army, but fatally detached himself with a small contingent to escort his wife back to the safety of Ladakh. On his return, a Sino-Tibetan force cut him off near Toyo, and his detachment was annihilated.

Such were the legends surrounding him that only a golden bullet was said to have brought him down. His

corpse was hacked into morsels to be hung up in local house-
holds, and even the hair of his body, which covered it 'like
eagles' feathers', was plucked out for luck. Every four years,
at the great monastery of Shepeling, his enshrined testicle
featured in a rare tantric rite, until the artillery of the
Cultural Revolution buried it. At Toyo a walled tomb once
enclosed the general's filleted bones, but when Indian pilgrims
visited in 1999 they found only rubble. Now the Tibetans
have reassembled its stones into a rough chorten, looped with
flags, where they still murmur mantras to the invader.

As we climb higher, the sky grows light and thin. The
streams peeling off Gurla Mandhata spread small, spinach-
green pastures before the wilderness returns. We pass a few
road builders' camps, and a castle turning to dust. In less
than an hour we have ascended 3,000 feet. Here and there a
monastery stands in the wastes, and nomad flocks are grazing on nothing under the far mountains. Then at 16,000 feet,
where the skyline is decked with cairns and flags, we crest
the Thalladong pass and veer to a stupefied halt. We are
gazing on a country of planetary strangeness. Beneath us,
in a crescent of depthless silence, a huge lake curves empty
out of sight. It is utterly still. In the plateau's barren smooth-
ness it makes a hard purity, like some elemental carving,
and its colour is almost shocking: a violent peacock blue.
There is no bird or wind-touched shrub to start a sound.
And in the cleansed stillness high above, floating on foothills
so faded that it seems isolated in the sky, shines the cone of
Mount Kailas.

In this heart-stopping moment pilgrims burst into cries
and prayer. Even our seasoned trekkers spill from their

Land Cruisers to gaze. There seem no colours left in the world but this bare earth-brown, the snow's white, and the sheen of mirrored sky. Everything else has been distilled away. The south face of Kailas is fluted with the illusion of a long, vertical stairway, as if for spirits to climb by. It shines fifty miles away in unearthly solitude. Void of any life, the whole region might have survived from some sacred pre-history, shorn of human complication. We have entered holy land.

Yet the lake is only precariously sacred. It is called Rakshas Tal, the lake of demons, and is inhabited by carnivor-ous Hindu spirits. Only one monastery, demol-ished in the Cultural Revolution, has ever touched its shores. Pilgrims shun it. Its crescent is imagined darker and more brooding than the holy lake of Manasarovar nearby, whose circle reflects the sun. It is said to be tormented by winds and ice floes, and to lie above drowned mountains. Its waters were once a dark poison. But a golden fish, swim-ming by chance out of Manasarovar, carved a channel into Rakshas by which the sunlit lake flowed into the black one and redeemed it. So, to the initiate, the moon-waters of Rakshas Tal become the dark complement – and psychic fulfilment – of Manasarovar.

We come down gently from the pass, and for a sterile moment the waters drop from sight. But minutes later another needle of blue – darker than the first – appears to our east, and we are descending to Manasarovar. As we pass a Hindu guest house, I feel a twinge of alarm that even in these soli-tudes this holiest of the world's lakes – sacred to one fifth of humankind – might have been polluted or built upon. Then it opens before us, untouched. Its waters yawn with the same fathomless intensity as Rakshas Tal, but the peacock blue has deepened to a well of pure cobalt, edged by snow mountains that overlook it from one horizon to another. At over 15,000 feet it is the highest freshwater lake of its size on earth. Two hundred square miles of water shine in its chain of snows, so that the few pilgrims who circumambulate it must walk for fifty-four miles. No life disturbs its waters as we descend. Only here and there breezes plough the surface with tracks, as if invisible ships had passed a minute before.

In fact no boat may sail here, and no one may fish its waters. There was a time when even hunting in this holy country was unknown. Visitors within living memory encountered bands of wild asses grazing — I glimpsed only one, shy and far away — and marmots and hares would watch innocently close at hand. In the past half-century, this has changed. But even now, as we reach lake level, a skein of geese flies in on an eerie rush of wings, and water birds are strutting and nesting a stone's throw away from where we pitch camp, and speckle the shore for miles.

From here, if you stand among the birds, the whole lake stretches into view. At its southern end the shelving ridges of Gurla Mandhata ebb still snowlit even along the eastern shore, while at the other end, beyond waves of brown foothills, Kailas mushrooms into the blue. These two white summits haunt the lake. Between them its indigo void appears coldly primeval. Tibetans call it Tso Mapham, 'the Unrivalled', or Rinpoche, 'the Precious'. Its hushed stillness seems to freeze it in a jewel-like concentrate of water. In both Buddhist and Hindu scripture the universe is born from such primal matter. A cosmic wind beats the water into worlds, and the god Vishnu, who dreams in the ocean near-eternally, creates diversity out of oneness by a sheer feat of will. Geology itself heightens the lake's strangeness. For Manasarovar is a stranded fragment of the Tethys Sea, almost drained by the upthrust of the Himalaya.

To Hindus, especially, the lake is mystically wedded to the mountain, whose phallic dome is answered in the vagina of its dark waters. Already in the second century the epic Ramayana, describing the Tibetan plateau, sites Kailas beside a great lake, beyond which spreads unending night. Manasarovar, they say, was created by the mind of God. It is the flower of first consciousness. In a time before scripture, a band of seers came here to worship Shiva, the god of destruction and change, who meditates on Kailas. To empower their ablutions, Brahma, the primal lord of creation, engendered from his thought these astral waters. The lake became the nursery of the gods. Sometimes Shiva floats here as a golden swan. At its centre, unseen by common eyes, the king of the serpents and his people feast on the Tree of Life, whose fruit turns golden and drops to the waters, infusing them with immortality. By the sixth century, in the classic Puranas, Manasarovar has become a full-blown paradise. From its roots in the serpent world below, the Tree overspreads the sky, and the lake is alive with bathing celestials and seraphic music.

It was in these pure waters that the Buddha's mother bathed before receiving him into her womb; and here the serpent king taught enlightenment to his *klu* water spirits, as Hindu and Buddhist traditions seamlessly fused. When the Buddha and his 500 flying disciples surfed in on their way to Kailas, the serpent disposed them on golden thrones over the lake, where Hindu swans were already singing.

These supernatural goings-on have left their trace along the shore. In the east it is streaked with curiously heavy pebbles, polished like gems. Behind us the pits abandoned in the slopes are the leftovers of gold prospectors, whose wounding of this sacred earth was punished by a plague of smallpox. It is said that a gold nugget shaped like a dog was dug up here a century ago, then returned to the earth in fear or piety. Holy lore has turned to magic all the lake's scanty life. Local people say that its herbs are sovereign against every disease, and when wave-battered fish are washed up dead on shore, the incense burned from them repels evil spirits. The lake's waters, drunk by the dying, usher the soul to paradise, and its sands inserted into a corpse's mouth prevent rebirth as an animal.

I walk like a pilgrim clockwise along the shore. The sun burns with a cleansing brilliance. The sands are grey and soft underfoot. At 15,000 feet the air feels light. My heart is beating harder, but my feet go numbly over the sand. The distances, in this clarified air, are greater than they seem. I make for a nearby headland, and two hours later I am still walking towards it. Objects look closer, but smaller, than they are. And solitary sounds – a faint cheeping and piping – only accentuate the silence. All along the waterline, between the lake's blank blue and the yellow land, coots and terns make a fringe of shifting life, tame in their borrowed sanctity. They never fly as I pass. Soon I am walking among whole colonies of water birds, as if invisible. Black-headed gulls mince in flocks along the shoreline; sandpipers pace the shallows and redshanks needle the soft earth alongside. Just offshore, pairs of Brahminy ducks are washing their coppery plumage and calling to one another in a soft, domestic two-note, then converge chuckling. I am tempted to wade in a little, where the crested grebes sit moored on their twig rafts. At ten yards their dagger beaks and black-plumed heads, splashed with Titian red, seem an arm's length away. Sometimes they dive suddenly, or call sadly at nothing.

As I round the headland a light wind rises, and miniature waves are breaking on the rocks. Just ahead, the promontory is heaped with white boulders that glisten unnaturally. In this dazzling air I feel oddly elated, unreal. Twenty miles away Gurla Mandhata silvers the water. At my feet slabs of stone have been prised upright and etched with prayers. What monks or pilgrims did this is impossible to know. The rock is chipped black around the words, which stand out in weathered ochre relief: *Om mani padme hum*, repeated like deep breathing. The slabs are canted mutely at the lake, or perhaps at Gurla Mandhata, home to the local rain goddess, and named from a legendary king who found salvation there.

High on the bluff above me ruined walls appear, and broken towers of loose-knit stones. I clamber up a slope of pure dust. There is nothing but wrecked rooms and the scent of artemisia. These, I realise, are the remains of Serkyi Cherkip, the Golden Bird monastery, where the Buddha and his disciples alighted to worship Kailas. It was gutted forty years ago in the Cultural Revolution. Until then eight small monasteries, roughly equidistant, had circled the lake like a mandala, each one symbolising a spoke of the Buddhist Wheel of Life. So pilgrims completing the lake's encirclement turned the wheel towards salvation. Six of these devastated monasteries have been restored, but they were never populous. At Cherkip, a century ago, the community had dwindled to a single monk. Morning and evening he rang its great bronze bell over the empty water, heard by no one.

It is Hindus who venerate the lake most deeply. Yet most of them gave up its *parikrama* – its ritual circuit – long ago. Perhaps because Manasarovar was born from the mind of Brahma, whose paradise is transient, they rather seek their final deliverance in Kailas, the abode of Shiva, whose worship leads them through incarnations to eternal peace. But they still bathe fervently in the lake's shallows, which release them from the sins of past lives.

Beyond the ruins I come upon a hundred-foot-long mani wall, cresting the bluff above the lake. Its slatey stones are layered pell-mell on a base of rocks, some of their prayers elaborately inscribed. Even the Red Guards, it seems, despaired of destroying this interminable mass, and monks had rescued the stones years later, fractured and whole together, then gone away. Now the stones spread strangely through the silence. Their slate is blue-grey, grey-green, smoother than a blackboard. Under their broken voices the waves are falling heavier on the headland now, and the wind hardening.

As I reach the promontory of white boulders, I realise they are not rocks at all, but hillocks of gleaming ice. I touch their congested cold, astonished. The June sun blazes down, and they are hard as steel. They might have been cast up from another age. I have forgotten that as late as May the whole lake is a battlefield of colliding ice. In winter the water level drops beneath a frozen carapace that periodically collapses under its own weight. Then the tumult freezes again, until the surface has splintered into a turquoise geometry of six-foot ridges. On shore, wrote the Indian swami Pranavananda, who studied the lake in winter seventy years ago, blinding snowstorms bury flocks and herds together, and wild asses die on all fours beneath the drifts. In the lake shallows, hundreds of fish lie frozen in transparent ice, and even swans perish with their cygnets, sandwiched by fracturing floes. A few days before it melts, the lake explodes into roars and groans, mixed with sounds like human cries and musical instruments. The icy slabs and prisms clash and heave upwards, and the surface yawns with six-foot cracks. Close to shore, ice blocks as big as fifty cubic feet are hurled from the lake to land yards inshore, still towering and erect, as on this worn headland, taller than I am, and mysteriously whole.

A mile from my camp, an isolated hill rises like a termites' nest. Its crags are disintegrating into scree, but around its crest the monastery of Chiu, 'the Little Bird', is plastered into clefts and caves, where its whitewashed chapels and cells look coeval with the rock. Stony paths and stairways meander about it, and strings of prayer flags, moored to cairns and boulders, billow from its summit like rigging in the wind.

A lean figure at the hill's foot turns out to be Ram, who has wandered here alone. He is gazing at the monastery in puzzlement or unease, so that I wonder what faith he follows. But he says: 'My people know nothing of religion. They are very poor.' His English comes shy and halting. 'They hardly know if they are Hindus or Buddhists. In my village it is all mixed.'

'You have no temple?'

'There is one lama started try to build a temple. He covered half of walls with *tanka*s, then no more money . . .'

His village is remote, he says, somewhere east of Everest, and his parents are old, his mother sixty-seven, his father sixty-two. 'My father is sick, with pains around his chest. But my mother very strong. They grow some barley and vegetables in exchange for rice. That is what we have.' He smiles hardily. 'And I have a little girl . . .'

'And your wife?'

'My wife is twenty-five.'

I say, half-laughing, as if to hide indelicacy: 'There is time for more children.'

But he answers gravely: 'No. We don't want more. We think one is enough. In Nepal families grow big, and it becomes hard to eat.'

Fleetingly I wonder at this unexpectedness: Iswor who will not marry until forty, Ram who does not want a son. The wind is stretching the prayer flags above us, the sun dipping. I say: 'Are you going into the monastery?'

But he only answers: 'There is nothing I want ask for,' and turns back.

A rough path winds among the prayer-hung crags and

fissures. I climb into a courtyard and a temple hall where a novice is chanting. A century ago the Swedish explorer Sven Hedin, examining the frescoes in Trugo monastery nearby, identified the muralled god of the lake, riding a pink horse, and the fish god rearing from the waves to greet him, his head gushing snakes and his body tapering to a dolphin's tail. But everything I see is new – no fresco has escaped the Red Guards – and the novice breaks off his prayer to usher me away and point out another path. It slides close under the crags. The lake below is darkening towards dusk, but Kailas is rising clear beyond it, and light clouds sailing above.

A monk emerges on the path in front of me, and waits. He is whiskered and frail, his face battered to teak by the wind. He opens a tin-bound gate labelled '2', which almost falls from its hinges. Beyond it a double door – startlingly rich – shines vermilion in the rock. Its leaves are bossed in brass and dripping with scarves. Beyond it, a now-familiar dark descends. I can barely see my way. The ceiling of the deepening cave falls close and soot-blackened. Lamps gutter in pools of isolated fire. Deep in his niche I can discern the gold glimmer of Padmasambhava, his hands clasping a thunderbolt.

This is his cave. It is believed that here, with his consort Yeshe Tsogyal beside him, Tibet's greatest saint passed the last seven days of his life in sacred trance. Then he 'took rainbow body', leaving behind only his hair and fingernails – and his faithful widow, who settled down to pen his biography. Beside me the old monk is murmuring and glaring half-blindly into my eyes, but I cannot understand him.

Once he gestures at a statue enshrined in the niche beside the saint and whispers: 'Yeshe Tsogyal!' But I make out only a shape painted dusty blue or grey, out of whose swathing pearls taper mandarin fingernails touched in blessing.

In this deepest recess of the cave, where the light has shrunk to a glimmer, the rock shape of a giant's footprint is hanging from the wall. Darkened by smoke and veneration, its stone glints faintly through the soil of pious hands. It seems to be dangling free from a ceremonial ribbon. But when I touch it, I realise it is an outcrop of the cave wall itself: shaped like a huge sandal. The monk has forgotten me, and is chanting at it with bewondered eyes. Padmasambhava, it seems, left such imprints all over Tibet, as if out of a sacred earth the stone recognised him.

He descends in a history florid with legend. In the eighth century, perhaps, he came from the Swat valley in today's Pakistan, where Buddhism already lay in ruins. In Tibet too, the older, Bon religion had regained the land, and Buddhism was fading. But popular histories are replete with Padmasambhava's miracles. Piously his life parallels the Buddha's. Born from a lotus, he is the adoptive son of a north Indian king, and attains enlightenment in exile, haunting the cremation grounds dear to tantric yogis. In Tibet he is tutored by the *dakini* sky-dancers. He traverses the mountains converting kings, war gods and devils alike. Twice he escapes immolation on pyres by turning them to water or sesame oil, appearing in the flames enthroned on a calm lake. The outsize hand- and footprints of his passing cover the land. An emanation, at last, of the Amitabha Buddha, he becomes immortal in death, and in a crescendo of attribution he leaves behind prescient treasure texts and writes the Book of the Dead.

The sect of Nyingma, the Ancient Ones, whose monastery I had visited at Yalbang, hail him as a second Buddha. It is he, they say, who retrieved the country's lost knowledge, and they who most rigorously guard it.

But as the histories grow earlier, so Padmasambhava fades. It seems he may stand in for a whole crowd of Indian yogis who reached Tibet around the eighth century. The monastery of Chiu, where I crouch beneath his sandal print, may be less than three centuries old. And in the earliest record of all, the saint dwindles to an itinerant water-diviner, who converted nobody.

None of this, of course, troubles the Kagyu monks who inhabit Chiu, any more than dubious saints disturb the Christian faithful. Slowly the old man leads me out of the cave where Padmasambhava meditated, or did not, and I put money on its altar. It is hard to know, from his aged face and tortoise movements, or from his brethren chanting in the temple, how wise or indolent these monks are.

For foreigners this has always been so. Long before the Chinese invasion, travellers recorded monasteries dulled by apathy and rote-learning. Over a century ago the Japanese monk Kawaguchi recoiled from their immorality (the scriptures were even used as lavatory paper, he said), and Swami Pranavananda, who visited some fifty monasteries over many years, mentioned only two lamas whom he esteemed.

But as the old man gazes at me, whispering and smiling, I long to know what he is saying. Western fantasies about Tibet's secret wisdom surface unbidden into my mind. His words rasp and fade. I stare hopelessly back at him. Is something important lurking behind those simple-seeming eyes? I question him in halting Mandarin, but he speaks none. I search for signs of use in the dusty tiers of scripture – the Kangyur and Tengyur – on the temple shelves; but they seem to be kept less for study than for veneration.

The tin door rattles shut behind me, and the monk is gone. The dusk is cold and clear. Below me I see the half-lit channel of Ganga Chu, carved by the golden fish as it made for Rakshas Tal. Its intermittent flow depends on the will of the serpent king, of course; it brings about the mystic intercourse of the lakes – or fails – and its fluctuation tells the future of Tibet. For thirty years after the Chinese invasion the channel was saline or bone dry. Now it oozes again beneath me in slow shallows out of Manasarovar, trickling to where Rakshas Tal lies palely to the west, but never arriving. Near its bed, the outlandish bubbling of hot springs has become a pilgrim bathhouse. But the channel's waters barely tremble. Brackish and uncertain, they idle unconsummated to the foot of a low dam.

This periodic flow was the bane of explorers hunting for the headwaters of the Indian rivers. Even now the source of the Sutlej, the giant tributary of the Indus, is variously placed here or at the rivulets seeping from the slopes southwest of Kailas. To Hindus especially such waters rise by divine intent, and in the ancient Puranas the four world rivers find their birthplace on the mystic slopes of Mount Meru. The holy Ganges itself descends from the sky, flowing through the locks of Shiva, or circles Brahma's heavenly city before splitting into four and flooding down from Meru to mankind.

By a freak of geography, which knit Kailas indissolubly to Meru, the four chief rivers of the Indian subcontinent rise within seventy miles of its summit. The Karnali, the highest source of the Ganges, has drifted to the west of us now, to find its birth beyond Rakshas Tal. Tibetans, who gave the rivers sonorous names, call it Magcha-Khambab, 'the River that flows from the Peacock's Mouth', while the Sutlej is Langchan-Khambab and flows from 'the Elephant's Mouth'. The Indus, the lion-mouth river, rises from scattered sources on the north flank of the Kailas massif itself, and the horse-mouth Brahmaputra in an obscure glacier a few miles to the east. These two titans then diverge along almost 2,000 miles each to clamp the whole Indian subcontinent in stupendous pincers. In their course they crash through the Himalaya in fearful gorges – the Brahmaputra falls through the deepest canyon on earth – then ease south into vast, slumbering estuaries. The Indus descends the length of modern Pakistan to the Arabian Sea, its waters still cloudy with the silt of Tibet and the Karakoram; the Brahmaputra spills into the Bay of Bengal after mingling with the Ganges among the mangroves and crocodiles of the world's widest delta.

The origin of these rivers baffled explorers for centuries. Ironically the first European to reach Kailas, the Jesuit Desideri, evaluated them more accurately than anyone who followed him for a century and a half (although he misplaced the source of the Ganges). Even the assiduous William Moorcroft was deceived by the vanishing channel of Ganga Chu.

But the explorer who bestrode the whole region was the remorselessly driven Sven Hedin. At once impelled and flawed by a lust for adulation, he cast himself in the mould of a sublime hero. He allowed nothing – not official prohibition, sub-zero temperatures nor the death of men and beasts – to divert his course. In 1907 he reached Manasarovar from the east after an illicit journey that filled in 65,000 square miles on the blank map of Tibet. Within a few weeks all but six of his hundred pack mules and ponies had perished. When at last he caught sight of the blue sheen of Manasarovar, he burst into tears. He spent a month on its shores in an investigative frenzy. To the dismay of the Tibetans, he assembled a cockleshell boat and launched on to the water. The god of the lake would pull him under, they said. They believed that at its centre Manasarovar bulged into a transparent dome, and that even if Hedin mounted it he would capsize in the waterfall beyond. Instead, he took soundings on both Manasarovar and Rakshas Tal, cruising for hours. He imagined himself the first to sail here. He knew nothing of the Scotsman whose debut in a rubber dinghy had caused the death of the local governor fifty years before.

When at last he returned to Europe, trumpeting his discovery of India's river sources, and of the mountains he named Trans-Himalaya, Hedin received a mauling from the society that had once most ardently supported him, the world's premier body of geographers, the Royal Geographic Society in London. He defended his claims with magisterial arrogance, and partial success. But only his siting of the Indus source proved indisputable (the Brahmaputra had been located by a jaunty British hunting party forty years before), and his mountains were redefined as a broken and nebulous massif unworthy of a Himalayan name.

In the cold British gaze Hedin had undermined his own achievements by exalting them. He retired to Stockholm, bruised and furious. He publicly supported Kaiser Wilhelm through the First World War, and Adolf Hitler in the Second, losing the love of his Swedish compatriots. He secured the release of several concentration camp victims, yet remained unrepentant of his Nazi sympathies. His fame darkened, and faded, and he died in near-obscurity in 1952, bequeathing his research to his estranged countrymen.

CHAPTER ELEVEN

· · · · · · ·

At night, the silence of the lake is pricked only by the faint cries of water birds in their sleep. The sky is white with stars, and with the waxing moon of Saga Dawa, the Buddhist holy month, which frosts our scattered camp. Hindus say the shooting stars are sky gods who descend to bathe in Manasarovar. An Indian pilgrim tells me later that her night was disrupted by flashing lights and strange cries.

Towards dawn I wake breathless to a world turned crimson. From one horizon to another the lake is a long slash of fire, and the sky lightening with lurid strata of red and pale gold. Easy to imagine this an apocalyptic fracture in the order of things, a portent of sacred chaos, or at least a fanfare for the dawning holy month. I stand outside my tent, distracted by some dream I have forgotten. Far to the south, over Gurla Mandhata, the clouds are congealed black, as if it were a zone of clogged, perpetual night, and all along the shoreline the grebes and sandpipers float or stand in the molten water, half of them still asleep.

The sky is paling to common day as I walk south along the littoral. Redshanks skitter about the sands, and the black-headed gulls fly back and forth and fuss in the shallows. Here and there the cliffs above me are pocked with caves. For centuries hermits have meditated around the lake, drawn to its lonely power. The whole region is riddled with their dwellings. I scramble up and find an entrance framed by rough-layered stones. Inside the cave is empty, but half ceilinged by timbers, and three votive scarves, quite new, hang on the rocks outside.

In the scarp above I glimpse a dwarfish doorway closed in plastered stones. A flurry of rock pigeons startles upwards as I clamber higher. The lake tilts and gleams below. A wafer-thin door swings in the cave entrance, once closed by a twist of wire that has dropped into the dust. As I edge it open, I feel suddenly uneasy. There are rumours of yogis still caverned round the lake – near Cherkip a solitary nun has only just left. I peer into half-darkness. I wonder momentarily if somebody has died here. By my hand a rusted stove is wedged deep in the cave wall, its chimney pipe wobbling up to a hole in the rock. But the cave is deserted. Its ceiling glints black like the vault of a coal mine. The smells are of dust, and the only noise is the sloshing of waves below. On a rock ledge deeper inside I come upon a bag of rice and another of salt, and a torch without a battery. Nearby lies a pouch of salinated earth, reverently gathered from the shores of the lake. Whoever was here, I realise, intended to return. But that, I think, was long ago.

The only clue hangs on a sheet of cardboard torn from a noodle carton propped against one wall. Some photographs of monks sag from its peeling sellotape, and beneath them dangles the notice of a 'heart return' ceremony in Nepal in the year 2000 for a Karmapa lama – 'Jamgon Kongtrul the Great' – who had passed into nirvana a century before.

So the hermit, perhaps, had belonged to the Kagyu sect, whose monks start meditating young, and which had once produced austere ascetics. I stare down from the cave entrance, imagining him climbing the cliff towards me, but the shore stretches empty. In such solitudes advanced yogis deepened their powers. And they were not precisely alone. Their discipline had been passed down, teacher to pupil, in long lineages of arcane knowledge, and all around them abandoned caves blazed with the holiness of their predecessors. Their near-magic practice arrived from India as early as the eighth century, and it became the heart of Tibetan faith. Their path was called *vajrayana*, the Thunderbolt or Diamond Vehicle, named from the hard swiftness with which it dispelled ignorance, and its scriptures were the esoteric texts named tantra. Its yogis – whether monk or layman – became a religious elite; but theirs was a dangerous and half-secret way. Within a single lifetime – a shockingly brief span to conventional Buddhists – the adept might overleap the toil of reincarnations and enter nirvana.

At times a belief that all experience – however mundane or immoral – could be channelled towards enlightenment licensed grotesque extremes. Matt-haired adepts haunted cremation grounds, pouring over themselves the dust of the dead, or sublimated taboos by orgiastic sex, downing alcohol and slaughtering animals. The world, after all, was illusory. Nothing was of itself impure. They could seem like licentious criminals. The Moghul emperor Akbar, most tolerant of rulers, had his tantric yogis torn to bits by elephants.

But the classic practice – however disrupted by Chinese persecution – involves a lone and rigorous self-transformation.

Guided by his guru, the novice selects a tutelary Buddha or divinity – a *yidam* – and by an intense practice of identification achieves an imagined fusion with him. It is this divinity, often, who is portrayed with his consort in the sexual union that the abbot of Yalbang had extolled: compassion joined with wisdom. Over months and years of rapt visualisation, the adept starts to assimilate to the *yidam*, enthroned, perhaps, in his mandala palace. As his mind awakens, he experiences the mandala as real. Sometimes the god himself may be conjured to inhabit it. In time the yogi can summon or dissolve the picture at will. And slowly, at will, he becomes the god. Mentally he takes on his appearance, his language (in oft-repeated mantras) and even his mind. He experiences his own body as a microcosm of the secret body of the universe. The world becomes a mandala. Seated upright, in union with Meru-Kailas, his breathing regulates and stills. At last he feels his body thinning into illusion, he merges with the Buddha, and it is time to depart.

'The world disappears. This is our peace.'

In his temple courtyard in Kathmandu, the genial monk Tashi, who had studied tantra for three years now, refused to call it a philosophy, still less a faith. 'We have no God.'

The gods were only guides to the enlightenment that would erase them. His arms unfolded impotently from his chest, trying to explain. 'I think it is a science. Anyone can do it. I think you can do it.'

I tried to imagine this, but the wrong words swam into my mind: rejected life, self-hypnosis, the obliteration of loved difference. Premature death. But tantrism was a way to be lived, Tashi said, not a doctrine to be learnt. You could not know it until you experienced it. Though by then, perhaps, it would be too late to return.

He said: 'In this meditation you find above all great strength, and eventual peace, the peace we all seek. Once you start out, yes, you know it will be foolish to give up. You will lose too much . . . nothing would be left.'

Soon he would be going into retreat for three years, and he longed for this. 'I could travel to my village in Bhutan and find a hut, but my family would give me no peace.' He laughed. 'I'd ask them to visit me just once a month, and they wouldn't understand . . .' So he did not know where he would go – that depended on his teacher – and in meditation it was this teacher he envisaged more than his *yidam*, imagining the man a Buddha. 'That is how it is with us. Even if your teacher is a poor one, you revere him.'

From the temple beside us the throb of prayer and the thud of drums reverberated like a strong heart. Compared to the shaped tunes of Christian chant, this deep, rhythmic muttering was not prayer at all, but an unearthly emanation. Then came the groan of the ten-foot horns, as if a great beast was stirring underground.

Tashi said suddenly: 'If I could come with you to Kailas, I would want to stay there. In that sacred place. Always. In solitude.'

I wondered then if hermits survived on Kailas, but Tashi did not know. 'But you will go there,' he said, 'and it will be good. It will clarify your mind, give you power. You will dedicate your pilgrimage to those who have died . . . and they will accrue merit.'

'They will?' My voice sounded harsh, wary of false consolation. 'Can you help the dead?' Some long-surrendered
faith in me recoiled. In my childhood, Anglicanism had
offered no Mass for the dead, no intercession. The dead
were beyond reach or comfort.

But for Tashi, the implacability of karma had been alle-
viated by kindlier traditions. 'Yes, dedicate good deeds to
them. If you go on such a journey with nothing in your
mind, it will be empty.'

Often he seemed very simple, very practical. He toler-
ated contradiction better than I did, I thought. Or perhaps,
for him, nothing contradicted. Sometimes he scratched his
head in amusement at something – his tonsure glossed it
like a tight helmet – and his fingernails made a noise like
tearing paper. After a while two cows wandered into the
courtyard from a nearby building site, and he went away to
coax them back.

From the hermit's cave above Manasarovar a skein of geese
flies silently at eye level eastwards. I climb down to the
shore again, where Kailas rises cloudless to the north. Floating above the steel horizon of the lake, the mountain has
guided generations of renunciates. Buddhists say its
guardian is the furious Demchog, whose ice palace is its
summit. He is portrayed as a raging demon, multi-armed
and skull-crowned, brandishing trident and drum, his
consort Phagmo twined fast about him. But this rampant
sentinel terrifies only the ignorant. He is not an indigenous
mountain god at all, but a tantric variant of Shiva, and his
mandala, complete with sixty-two attendant goddesses, is

Kailas itself. So the god fades into his own mountain, and the mountain owns him.

The shape of Kailas – a near-perfect cone thrusting from the mist – may have attracted veneration in a time of primitive fertility worship, long before the Aryan invasions of 1500 BC. Later Hindu scriptures likened the peak to a tumescent penis or an oozing breast. Yet the early Aryans feared its future god, Shiva, as the outcast lord of renegades and thieves. The first epics – the Ramayana, the Mahabharata – place him only tentatively on Kailas, and celebrate Mount Meru as a separate, mystic country. The Himalaya then were divine territory, feared by mortal men, and few but ascetics dared penetrate them from the plains. But to follow the rivers to their source was to seek out holiness, and the rivers led to Kailas. Some time early in the second millennium, Shiva was enthroned here in a surge of Hindu piety. Mount Meru broke into the human world, converging with Kailas, and multiple paradises radiated over the slopes. Tiers of gods and spirits ascended the mountain in an ever more powerful elite. Its scarps flowered with jewels, herds of sacred elephants barged through its sandalwoods, and its air rang with celestials' song. On its lower planes the caves gleamed with the piety of hermits, and in fragrant forests the souls of the dead awaited rebirth. The mountain enfolded all extremes. From caverns beneath it, grim titans emerged to do battle with the gods, and the abyss of hell yawned below.

Shiva, meditating on the mountain's summit, retains the shadow of his renegade past. He is the lord of havoc and regeneration, patron of mystics and wanderers. His face is smeared blue with the ash of the dead. He dances the world into being, and into ruin again. He brings both the hope and the desolation of change. Only the yogi can still this impermanence, who in trance imagines his body united with Meru-Kailas, and who activates its psychic energies until they float him into peace.

In early scripture Parvati, daughter of the mountain god Himalaya, seeks out Shiva and seduces him over thousands of years, by her ascetic devotions and immortal beauty. She becomes his *shakti*, his energising genius, and their marriage on the mountaintop is the union of thought and untamed nature. But Parvati is as changeable as he. Sometimes she is called Urna, pure light. At others she is Kali, the terrible goddess whose sacrifices had drenched my feet at Dakshinkali.

Whoever its presiding divinity, the concept of a world mountain pervaded Asia. A shadowy etymology even links Meru to ancient Sumer and the ziggurats of Babylon. Hindu temples were planned to emulate the mountain's mystic layout – for they too are the dwellings of gods. The great eighth-century Kailasa temple at Ellora, carved from living basalt, is a conscious mirror of Meru, as is the third-century BC Buddhist stupa at Sanchi. In the Shaivite sanctuaries of south India, especially, the roofs beetle skywards in multi-tiered mountains, and their ritual water tanks echo Manasarovar. In Tibet itself the chortens are miniature Merus, while the white triangle of Kailas is daubed on countless cottage doorways. In south-east Asia the Cambodian Khmer raised their massive temples on the same pattern – Angkor Wat is a giant image of Meru – and the

Meru-shaped palaces of the Burmese kings helped to sanctify their tyranny.

Two years after my father's death, while distracting my mother with a tour of Java, we reached the largest Buddhist monument in the world. Barely a century before, the temple mountain of Borobudur had lain among volcanic ash and jungle, but now it lifted its worn stones free in nine immense, sculptured terraces to a crowning spire. We circled its galleries in wonder, their carvings enigmatic to us. Its lower tiers seemed to portray earthly life and the legends of the Buddha, but as we ascended, the bas-reliefs turned unknown. We were straying up the flanks of a vast cosmic symbol. In its concentric mass, tiered purposively from earth to nirvana, lava or jungle had preserved its panels almost pure. You read them right to left, circling clockwise, as if up some delicate initiation. This was the universe in stone imagined by the eighth-century Sailendra dynasty, 'lords of the mountains'. Sometimes my mother paused, panting. I did not know then that in youth she had strained her heart. She never spoke of it. Perhaps she herself had forgotten. But now, in old age, its fibrillation was shortening her breath.

But she joked, in holiday mood, that we were ascending to enlightenment. On the top terrace we looked out on misted jungle, and her breathing stilled. Along these esplanades some seventy Buddhas sat in cages of latticed stone, gazing outwards. 'So this is nirvana . . .' She spoke as if inspecting somewhere fascinating but irrelevant. She might have asked (but did not) if nirvana held the tang of interesting troubles, or Dalmatians, or those she loved. Beneath us the jungle bloomed rich on volcanic earth. After a while she took my hand and asked to go down again.

The clarity of the air draws the figure closer than he is. I glimpse him, black and sharp-edged – a Hindu pilgrim, knee-deep in the lake – and see the glitter of water as he splashes his face. By the time I reach his headland he is gone. A sodden prayer book is lying on the sand, and in the waves floats a tiny votive sheaf tied with string, which I cannot touch.

Close by, sixty years ago, some of Mahatma Gandhi's ashes were scattered over the lake. Hindus more than Buddhists bathe in the icy water, drink it, carry it away. Its purifying powers deepen in their scriptures, until it washes away the sorrow of all mortal beings. To bathe in it is to be destined for Brahma's paradise; to drink it redeems the sins of a hundred lives.

Close to shore the water comes oddly warm to my touch. The Hindu Puranas ask that pilgrims here pour out a libation to the shades of their forefathers. This rite of *tarpan*, it is said, eases their souls into eternity.

As I wade a few yards into the shallows, they turn cold. I cup the water in my hands. I feel a momentary, bracing emptiness. But the *tarpan*'s truth is not mine. Its dead are changed into other incarnations, or faded in eternity.

In a celebrated passage of the Bhagavad Gita, Krishna addresses Arjuna the archer before battle: *Thou hast mourned those who should not be mourned* . . . It is impossible, he implies, to terminally kill or die. People shed one life for another.

Nor at any moment was I not,
Nor thou, nor these kings.
And not at all shall we ever come not to be . . .

So the two warriors pass into battle and hew down men with the exalted half-smile of Hindu gods. For they know they are killing nothing of importance. The erasure of the individual is the condition of salvation.

I still my feet in the cold water. I want to call out a name, but flinch from the expectation of silence. In these waters of Hindu consolation, people as I know them are extinguished. Like Borobudur, the lake is immense, primordially alien. I hug myself against an imaginary wind. A tightness opens in my stomach. I want to touch hands that I know have gone cold. The air feels thin.

Where are you? Among the graves of an English church-yard – so many I don't know – my breaking voice reminds me of someone else's. It is, of course, of yours. You exist now in the timbre of my voice.

The bar-headed geese are flying again along the sands, and seem uncertain where to go. Beyond them the white folds of Gurla Mandhata balloon over the water. Farmers in the lower Indus valley, watching the geese take the river passage north to Manasarovar in spring, imagine they are heading for paradise. Perhaps these are the royal swans whose plumage, some say, turns to gold. Pilgrims are enjoined to worship them as Shiva, before pouring out water to the past.

CHAPTER TWELVE
· · · · · · ·

In 1715 the Jesuit missionary Ippolito Desideri, travelling from Kashmir towards Lhasa, passed 'a mountain of excessive height and great circumference, always enveloped in cloud, covered with snow and ice, and most horrible, barren, steep and bitterly cold . . . The Tibetans walk devoutly round the base of the mountain, which takes several days, and they believe this will bring them great indulgences. Owing to the snow on this mountain, my eyes became so inflamed that I well nigh lost my sight.'

He was the first known Westerner to set eyes on Kailas, where he nearly saw nothing more. Few who came after him were not moved. Even to mundane eyes its beauty was tinged with strangeness. Its apparent cone is in fact a steep pyramid, and each side faces a cardinal compass point. To the excitement of geologists, its mass is not Himalayan gneiss but an ancient Tertiary gravel lifted on granite: the highest such deposit in the world. For Kailas is the lonely relic of an age still earlier than the Himalaya, and was once the highest island in the dwindling Tethys Sea. As summer advances, the melting snows on the south face break across its illusory stairway to sketch a shadowy swastika. This venerable symbol – so corrupted in the West – recurs as a sign

143

of good fortune all through India and beyond. In Tibet it survives alongside its more ancient opposite (whose arms hook backwards), and on the flank of Kailas it flowers like a portent.

As our Land Cruiser crosses the Barga plain towards the base of the mountain – in lumbering convoy with the British trekkers – there is no sign yet of any swastika, nor even of the lesion circling the mountain's foot, inflicted by demons trying to drag it away. All around us the foothills are scribbled with juniper scrub, and the plain is newly green, where herds of horses drift. From time to time we see hearthrugs moving over the slopes. With quaintly hunched shoulders and bushy culottes, these are yaks. In their darkly dripping coats they stand out like rocks against the bleached grass where they graze, and we plan to hire one to replace Dhabu and Pearl. Once too I glimpse a lone goral – a Himalayan goat-antelope – wandering across the plateau, delicate and pale, as if lost.

As we draw closer, the mountain's strangeness intensifies. The whole massif to its east leans faintly towards it, flowing in brown waves to the white pyramid under a wash of blue sky. Slowly we are approaching the settlement of Darchen, where pilgrims hire beasts for the mountain circuit. Here, traditionally, is the start of the pilgrimage. A century ago Kawaguchi found it a cluster of thirty stone houses. A curious treaty assigned its administration to the Maharaja of Bhutan, together with many local monasteries, but when a visiting British trade commissioner arrived in 1905, he found everybody drunk. Twenty-one years later his successor found everybody still drunk. Thirty years ago, in the wake of the Cultural Revolution, the place was all but abandoned, emptied by persecution and winter storms. The only inhabitants were a deranged Tibetan couple who lived in the chapel of the decaying monastery.

From the military checkpoint that stops us short of it, Darchen looks ordered and compact. In twenty years it has become a town. But as we approach, it starts to fall apart. Its buildings separate down stony streets, which peter out uphill. We arrive at an open space where a few alleys converge. It is strewn with trash and broken stones. A wavering line of shops is here, Chinese and Tibetan side by side, where I buy some beer then wander the town in dismay. I pass run-down guest houses, Chinese army compounds, a leftover monastery. A lifeline of prayer flags loops over a squalid gully to the foot of the mountain. Meanwhile our alien permits are scrutinised by police, who at last ratify them, but any attempt to hire yaks is doomed. It is the eve of Saga Dawa, when pilgrims converge on Kailas, and the region has run out of yaks. The town is uneasy. It is over a year since the pre-Olympics riots in Lhasa, but the Chinese distrust of gatherings is running high. Access to this remotest province is always hard, but police have constricted it further, for fear of a huge congregation under the mountain.

Yet the pilgrims are filtering in. They trail curiously about the shops, shadowed by their tousled children, their gear heaped on their backs. The men go anonymous in assorted caps and anoraks, and I cannot tell how far they have come. But the sheepskin *chuba*s of the women fall to their feet beneath aprons striped scarlet, green and oxblood red, and their hair hangs braided to the waist under scarves and little ear-flapped bonnets. When their faces are not masked against the dust, they are smiling.

A shopkeeper speaking mixed Mandarin and English tells me the town has grown more bitter. Three years ago, he says, a thirty-foot statue of Padmasambhava was raised on a nearby hill with the help of local monasteries. 'In fact we all gave money for it. I paid money myself.' He grimaces. 'Then they put a cord round its neck and pulled it down.' He whispers: 'The Chinese army, of course.'

Their tread is heavy. We are close to a border disputed with India, and the barracks sprawl. From time to time squads of soldiers wielding batons and riot shields stamp through the streets, their march an open threat yet faintly absurd, their arms bullying wide. Camp followers are here too. Sad, rough women emerge beside me wheedling *amo, amo*, so that I wonder for a moment if they speak Italian, then remember the Mandarin for massage.

A huge wall of mani stones and whitewashed stupas marks where the pilgrimage begins, its parapets and towers festooned with flags and piled with yaks' skulls. Round this derelict-looking monument the circling devotees are mostly ancient, too frail for the kora, the mountain circuit itself. Instead they hail the holy month by this creeping ambulation, murmuring an *Om mani padme hum* with every bead that drips from their blackened fingers. Sometimes they chant longer prayers, distressed or musical, flattening their palms together in still graceful supplication, or twirl hand-held prayer wheels. In the stupas the apertures are clogged with tiny clay Buddhas left by votaries to guide the dead, and the yak skulls are heaped even on nearby ledges. Between the black horns the bone blazes with mantras steering the beasts to a better afterlife, or inscribed in penance for their deaths.

We skirt the slope beyond, Iswor and I, shaking the dust of Darchen from us. Kailas is out of sight, hidden by dark outcrops. On a track below, still travelled by Land Cruisers and army lorries, Ram and our tents have preceded us to where the pilgrims are gathering for Saga Dawa. On this first, desultory stretch of the kora not a soul is in sight. A dry wind is flailing the rocks. For a hundred yards a mani wall follows our path along the flank of the hills, its stones all canted at the mountain, unbroken. To the south float the snows of Gurla Mandhata – with the spectral peaks of Saipal and Api beyond in Nepal – and flat-bottomed clouds are cruising the sky.

A single pilgrim appears marching far ahead of us, but faster than us, and vanishes. Once we come upon a rank of bronze prayer wheels turning in emptiness, and circle it happily. I had imagined such wheels contained paper leaves that fluttered loose when turned, but on this wind-hacked slope several have cracked open and I see inside – guiltily, as if glimpsing intestines – the pristine prayers coiled tight in cylindrical wads.

A stone flies into Iswor's eye. We bathe it from my water bottle beside the lonely prayer wheels. Tortoiseshell butterflies dither about us. Then we start again, tramping over dry gullies. The way is flagged by cairns of ivory-white stones cast up by the conglomerate mountain, cairns to which pilgrims add a pebble in passing. By these we are gently ascending. We pass a stone pile more huge than normal. Then the poles of prayer flags, felled by the winds perhaps years ago, lie across our approach like a shattered stockade. Here at last, by a little plateau, Kailas swings clear of its own massif. The black, toppling ziggurat of a hill still intervenes, but beyond this, out of its dun foothills, the white summit moves up like the cone of a rocket. Here we stand at the first *chaksal gang* of the kora, a platform for ritual prostration, facing the mountain. It is strewn with whatever anyone can carry up: inscribed stones, yak horns, articles of clothing. But the pilgrims have gone before us. It is so quiet that the loudest noise is the buzzing of bees among the fallen flags. This sacred wreckage of skulls, stones and garments looks organic with the rocks where it lies. I sit on a boulder, waiting for someone to come, but nobody does. Iswor stares at the emerging mountain, one hand over his eye. The pale horizons of the Barga plain have been squeezed from sight behind us. An hour later we are descending to the holy valley of the Lha river, which flanks Kailas west and north. The canyon walls climb dark and serrated along it, and the wind has fallen.

We come over a hill to an amphitheatre of worn grass. An espalier of linked flags surrounds it, converting the valley to a vast, open-ended oval of suspended and dripping colour. In the centre an eighty-foot pole – three or four pine trees clamped end to end – hovers stupendously aslant, waiting to be raised tomorrow, and around it the crowds are already processing clockwise, several hundred of them, chanting.

But an apprehension is in the air. The lorries of the

Chinese police and army have penetrated along the valley – they are lined up opposite us – and every twenty yards, in a cordon round the pole, a soldier is standing stolidly to attention. The police are sealing off an overhanging hillock, and the truncheon-wielding squads are tramping back and forth. But beyond the palisade of flags, the pilgrims camp oblivious among boulders, picnicking or praying. Traders have set up shop in tents, and a Chinese mobile clinic is processing people for swine flu.

The only building is a stone hut. Cramped into its dimness, seated at low tables, some twenty Kagyu monks are chanting and playing instruments. The noise is terrific. They are robed in a medley of crimson, maroon and mustard yellow, and they span all ages. The emblazoned hats of the senior monks taper up like cherry-red mitres, while the juniors' flare into pharaonic crowns that overhang their faces a foot above. They motion me to sit with them. Their tables are littered with butter lamps, bells, bottles of cola, and the stiff leaves of sutras. Aligned in worship, they form a genial gallery of whiskered age and callow youth. Mostly their hair is cropped or bound in pigtails, but sometimes their cheeks drizzle beards and wispy sideburns, and their locks fly free around spectacles glimmering in stranded orbs. I wonder if it was one of these Kagyupa who took refuge in the hermit's cave above Manasarovar, and rejoiced at the lama's 'heart return'.

Pilgrims crowd in, touching money to their foreheads before they leave it for the monks. A novice collects the notes in a box labelled *Budweiser*, while another ducks among the chanting heads to serve them supper – bowls of coagulated

149

rice and radishes – which they eat with jovial slurping while they pray. And all the time the unearthly music continues, with its voices like insects stirring, the horns braying their melancholy, the tap of a curved stick on an upright drum, and the watery explosion of cymbals.

It was this Red Hat sect, in the twelfth century, that instigated around Kailas the practice of sky burial. Perhaps, as some say, the Tibetans' is a death-haunted culture. Certainly their death cults haunt others. When I escape from the clamour of the monk-filled hut, I see before me, above the ground where the enormous pole will rise tomorrow, an empty plateau against the valley wall. On this Drachom Ngagye Durtro the sky burial of monks and nomads continues. The remorseless god Demchog, who dances out on Kailas the promise and terror of dissolution, imbues the Durtro with an ambivalent power. Like Shiva, whose ash-blue skin and skull garlands he shares, Demchog is lord of the charnel house, and his followers in the past have inhabited cremation grounds (they occasionally still do) to meditate on the impermanence of life and achieve the truth of emptiness. It is to such places, especially in this propitious month of Saga Dawa, that people may go to lie down and enact their own passing. So the *durtros* become sites of liberation. Rainbows link them to the eight holiest cremation grounds of India, whose power is mystically translated to Tibet.

A land of frozen earth, almost treeless, can barely absorb its dead. Holy law confines to burial only the plague-dead and the criminal: to seal them underground is to prevent their reincarnation and to eliminate their kind for ever. The corpses tipped into Tibet's rivers are those solely of the destitute. Embalmment is granted to the highest lamas alone, while the less grand are cremated and their ashes encased in stupas.

For the rest, the way is sky burial. For several days after clinical death, the soul still roams the body, which is treated tenderly, washed by monks in scented water and wrapped in a white shroud. A lama reads to it the Liberation by Hearing, known in the West as the Tibetan Book of the Dead, by which the soul is steered towards a higher incarnation. An astrologer appoints the time of leaving. Then the corpse's back is broken and it is folded into a foetal bundle. Sometimes this sad packet – surprisingly small – is carried by a friend to the sky burial site, sometimes it is laid on a palanquin and preceded by a retinue of monks, the last man trailing a scarf behind him to signal to the dead the way they are going.

As the corpse approaches, the sky master blows his horn, and a fire of juniper twigs summons the vultures. The master and his *rogyapa* corpse-dissectors then open the body from the back. They remove the organs, amputate the limbs and cut the flesh into small pieces, which they lay nearby. The bones are pulverised with a rock. The master mixes their dust with yak butter or *tsampa,* roasted barley, and then rolls it into balls. Finally the skull too is smashed and becomes a morsel with its brains. One by one these are tossed on to a platform – the bones first, for they are the least appetising – and the vultures crowd in.

These birds are sacred. On the burial platform above me

they are thought to be emanations of white *dakinis*, the peaceful sky-dancers who inhabit the place. Their fore-knowledge of a meal is uncanny. In his journals my father noted the mysterious speed with which they congregated, and speculated that they signalled to one another in flight by some system of their own. The submission of a corpse to them is the last charity of its owner, and lightens the karma of the dead. The birds themselves are never seen to pollute the earth. They defecate in the sky. Tibetans say that even in death they keep flying upwards until the sun and wind take them apart.

As I climb to the Durtro plateau, it shows no sign of life. A healing spring flows near its foot, and a white segment of Kailas shines above. My path winds up into light-blown dust. Beside me the cliff is the colour of old rose, scored by vertical cracks. The sun is dipping as the way levels into an aerial desolation. It is scattered with inchoate rocks, which may be those of rude memorials, makeshift altars, or of nothing. An icy wind is raking across it. The slabs for dis-section are merely platforms, smoothed from the reddish stone and carved with mantras. People have left hair and clothing here, even teeth and fingernails, like hostages or assents to their death. I see a woman's silk waistcoat, and a child's toy. Some of the boulders are clumsily clothed. A folded stretcher lies abandoned. And now the wind is wrenching at all ephemera and bundling it away – faded garments, old vulture feathers, tresses of hair – to decay at last under rock shelves.

For a while I see nobody but an old couple wandering the perimeter. They move as if blind, huddled against the cold.

Then I become aware of a man lying prostrate fifty yards away. As I look, he gets to his feet and hurls handfuls of *tsampa* into the wind, crying out. I make out a young face, circled in black locks. The wind stifles his words. He seems to be praying not to Kailas – his back is turned to it – but to the cemetery itself. Perhaps he is addressing the *dakini*s, but more likely he is invoking the *gompo*s, the Dark Lords who inhabit all cemeteries. The followers of these *gompo*s are the dregs of the spirit world: the hungry ghosts, the flesh-eaters, the *rolang* undead. By the rite of *chodpa* the yogi invites them to devour his ego, hurrying him to salvation. And suddenly the man's *tsampa* has finished and he is rolling in the dust. His hair spins about him. He makes no sound. This is no pious grovel but a headlong rotation over the ground, inhaling the dead. Then he lies still.

After he leaves, I go over to the terrace where he had been. Among the boulders I see two long, wide-bladed knives, then the ashes of a fire where a charred hacksaw lies. Then I come with alarm to the centre of the platform. A wooden board is there, scarred by blades. There are other knives, quite new, and an axe. They seem to have been discarded. And beneath the board, two bones are lying together – the arm bones of a human – with dried blood and flesh still on them.

I walk away. I feel a wrenching revulsion, and a shamed excitement at the forbidden. I had heard that sky masters were artists of their kind, heirs to a strict profession. To leave one human piece uneaten will invite demons into the body: they will reanimate it as a *rolang*, a living corpse, and steal its spirit.

But everything on the Durtro betrays crude carelessness. Perhaps its sky master has grown bitter. As with butchers and blacksmiths, the stench of uncleanness clings to these *rogyapa*s. Called 'black bones', they are shunned in their community. If one should eat in your home, his plate is thrown away. Their daughters rarely marry. Sometimes, too, their rules are transgressed. Tantric yogis even now, seeking stuff by which to brood on death, find human thigh bones for their trumpets, and skulls are offered them as ritual cups.

I cross the plateau in numb recoil. Only a belief in reincarnation might alleviate this bleak dismay. Without it, the once-incarnate dead become uniquely precious, and break the heart.

At sky burials the grief of relatives is said to disrupt the passage of the soul, and sometimes none attend. Instead a monk is sent in advance to the cemetery, to ask its spirits to comfort the corpse as its body is dismembered. But generally the mourners come: it is important, they may think, to confront evanescence, and witness liberation. At some funerals, so onlookers claim, the mourners display no sorrow. They have learnt the lesson of impermanence, and look with equanimity at the passing of the appearances they know.

But others say they lie on the ground, weeping.

Ram has pitched camp by the Lha river, where the humped tents of German and Austrian trekkers – arrived overland from Lhasa – seem suddenly a multitude beside us. Everybody is hunting for yaks or *jhaboo*s or ponies to carry their baggage, and perhaps themselves, around the mountain. But all these beasts are too few. And the kora confronts us with another 3,500-foot ascent, much of it steep. Iswor and I decide to jettison everything superfluous tomorrow and carry a single tent, with iron rations.

Late that night I wake to the soft, insistent ring of a mobile phone. I grope outside into the dark, listening for its source. But the nearest tent is out of earshot, and now there is no more sound. I wait, suddenly desolate. I feel sick at some imagined loneliness. Someone was trying to reach me, and I did not answer. Perhaps it is the hallucinatory shortage of oxygen, the starved brain, that summons this dream, and its incommensurate sadness.

I try to dispel it by walking. The Saga Dawa moon is full and shining on the river, and the sky dense with stars. In this thin air their constellations multiply and blur together like mist. The orange ones are probably long dead, their light arriving in posthumous and detached rays out of nowhere, while others are being born invisibly in the dark.

CHAPTER THIRTEEN

. . . .

The pilgrims circling the flagpole in the valley might be mimicking the greater kora of Kailas. They must ritually keep sacred objects on their right, so they orbit clockwise from early morning, in an aura of triumph. Viewed from the hillock where I stand, this seems an act not only of faith but of possession, as tigers mark out their territory at night, and I have the notion that Tibetans, by repeated holy circuits – of mountains, monasteries, temples – are unconsciously reclaiming their sacred land.

Whether in the ritual of pilgrimage, the cycles of reincarnation or the revolution of the Buddhist Wheel, the circle is here the shape of the sacred. In folklore, gods, demons and even reptiles perform the kora. By this dignity of walking (and in Tibetan speech a human may be an 'erect goer' or 'the precious going one'), pilgrims acquire future merit and earthly happiness, and sometimes whole families pour round Kailas with their herds and dogs – all sentient creatures will accrue merit – after travelling here for hundreds of miles.

As the morning wears on, the crowds thicken. A thousand pilgrims there may be, wheeling round the mast like planets round a sun. They go fast, buoyantly, as if on pious holiday. In this biting air the sheepskin coats still dangle from their shoulders in ground-trailing sleeves; the ear flaps fly free from women's bonnets, and the men's shaggy or cowhand hats are tilted at any angle. Sometimes, in ragged age, the people prod their way forward with sticks, their prayer wheels spinning. Among them the tribal nomads march in a multi-coloured flood. All that the women have seems on display, and a playful courtship is in the air. Their belts are embossed silver and seamed with cowrie shells, and sometimes dangle amulets or bells. They are bold and laughing. Necklaces of amber and coral cluster at their throats, their brows are crossed by turquoise-studded head-bands and their waists gorgeously sashed. There are groups of local Dropka herdspeople, and hardy Khampas from the east, whose hair is twined with crimson cloth. And here and there gleam fantastical silk jackets – pink, purple and gold, embroidered with dragons or flowers.

Ringed by Chinese soldiers, the flagpole stays monstrously aslant, dripping with prayer flags, waiting. The celebratory pennants fly everywhere, in colours too synthetic for the elements they symbolise, their yellow brighter than any earth, their green too vivid for water. Examining them, I recognise only Padmasambhava, stamped in woodblock, and the sacred wind horse, saddled with holy fire. On the outmost perimeter other prayers hang in faded waterfalls, printed on white cloth twice the height of a man. Bundled into diaphanous swags, they fall massed and unreadable, like folded books. But every year they are assembled here, their draped forms fidgeting like ghosts in the wind, to bestow the protection of their sutras, the magic of words.

On a hillock above, the police scan the valley through binoculars, and officers are coordinating patrols through a walkie-talkie. Their telescopic video camera whirrs on a tripod, waiting to record troublemakers. The soldiers remain at attention in their cordon round the pole and other squads – swinging truncheons and riot shields – swagger anticlockwise against the pilgrims or stand in units of five or six beyond the hanging prayers. But the Tibetans look straight through them, as if they had no meaning. All morning a helmeted Chinese fire officer stands alone and rigid, fulfilling some regulation, with a canister on either side of him and nothing flammable in sight.

The northern clouds have thinned away, and the tip of Kailas rises beyond the charnel ground. A few pilgrims are facing it now, lifting their joined hands to their foreheads. They call the mountain not the Sanskrit Kailas but Kang Rinpoche, 'the Precious One of Snow'. They may imagine on its crest the palace of Demchog, but even this Buddhist blessing cannot quite dispel a sense of ancient and impersonal sanctity, as if the mountain's power were inherently its own. This is the stuff of magic. In the eyes of the faithful its mana is intensified wondrously through all those who have meditated here, so that the kora is rife with their strength. A single mountain circuit, it is said, if walked in piety, will dispel the defilement of a lifetime, and bring requital for the murder of even a lama or a parent, while 108 such koras lift the pilgrim into Buddhahood.

These mathematics weigh the mountain's magic against the pilgrims' spirit. In the past the rich might pay a proxy to undertake the circuit, the virtue dividing between them; and even now, if a pilgrim rides a yak or pony, half the merit goes to the beast. Both yak and human are subject to earthly contamination, *drib*, which like a stain or shadow accumulates alongside outright sins. Pilgrimage cleanses these. The way of tantric meditation, which dismantles the illusions of difference, is only for the few, and those around me, slowed now to gaze at the raising of the pole, will rack up merit by an earthier journey tomorrow.

A century ago Sven Hedin, the first Westerner to complete the kora, wrote that its pilgrims' motives were simple. They hoped in a future life to be allowed to sit near Demchog; but they had other, more material concerns. Even now the remote workings of karma fade before the day-to-day. The pilgrim prays for disease to leave his cattle, for a higher price for his butter, for luck in sex or gambling. She wants a radio, and a child. Such matters belong to the Buddhas and tutelary spirits of a place. In the lonely hermitages, the *gompa*s, around Kailas, they will offer the spirits incense to smell, a little rice to eat, a bowl of pure water. And somewhere in these wilds they may whisper to the fierce mountain gods to bring back the Dalai Lama to Lhasa, and drive the Chinese out.

A slight, saffron-clad figure stands before the flagpole. Tiny and quaint under a tasselled crimson hat, he is the master of ceremonies, piping orders through a megaphone. Two hefty gangs, thirty strong each, start heaving on long ropes attached high up the mast, while a pair of lorries, their front bumpers bound to it by cables, go slowly into reverse. A shout of expectation goes up, and paper prayers are hurled into the wind. The pole begins to lurch upwards. The rods that have supported it aslant drop away, and its strands of tethered prayer flags are dragged upwards in harlequin arcs. Then the pole judders to a stop, hanging at a forty-five-degree diagonal, like a gun barrel pointing at Kailas. The spectators are shouting in a tense half-chant, their hands clasped together. The master of ceremonies runs from side to side, guiding the rope gangs. If the pole does not slot bolt upright in its socket of stones, ill luck will befall Tibet for the coming year. For two decades until 1981 the ceremony was banned, while the country suffered. And now the guy ropes are taut and equal, the saffron figure shouts, and the pole glides upwards until all support is gone. The carnival streamers unfurl like petals around it, and the great tree stands miraculously upright, held only by these frail garlands of colour. The sky-blue silk at its summit, by design or chance, slips down to reveal the golden orb that crowns it, and the crowd bursts into triumphant cries of *Lha-gyel-lo-so-so! Lha-so-so! Lha-so-so!* Victory to the gods! They shower fistfuls of *tsampa* into the air, over and over, exploding it in pale clouds towards the mountain. They delve into bags brimming with prayer leaves, which soon become a snowstorm. A ceremonial oven, built of clay brick and stoked with yak dung and juniper, becomes a repository for more thrown prayers and incense sticks, until the air fills with a dense white blossom of benediction – scent, blown barley, paper – that falls round the boots of the Chinese soldiers, still impassively at attention, and floats on like mist towards Kailas.

At this moment something strange happens. High above, on the rim of the charnel ground, a white-robed figure raises a wooden cross. He descends towards us like a mystic Christ returning from Calvary, a tiny Buddhist monk fussing behind him, and vanishes into the crowds. But soon this enigma is lost among the pilgrims, who are revolving again like a great coloured wheel around the flag-fluttering tree, infectiously happy. Some reach its foot to touch their foreheads to its stem; others have thrown themselves on the stony earth, their arms stretched towards the mountain, palms joined. Even the police are photographing one another.

The monks, who have been praying in a seated line for hours, advance in a consecrating procession. Led by the abbot of Gyangdrak monastery from a valley under Kailas, they move in shambling pomp, puffing horns and conch shells, clashing cymbals. Small and benign in his thin-rimmed spectacles, the abbot holds up sticks of smouldering incense, while behind him the saffron banners fall in tiers of folded silk, like softly collapsed pagodas. Behind these again the ten-foot horns, too heavy to be carried by one monk, move stertorously forward, their bell-flares attached by cords to the man in front. Other monks, shouldering big drums painted furiously with dragons, follow in a jostle of wizardish red hats, while a venerable elder brings up the rear, cradling a silver tray of utensils and a bottle of Pepsi-Cola.

But by late afternoon, with the ceremonies over, the wheeling crowds have thinned away. All round the perimeter they have looped the circling flags inwards to the pole, so that walking here you clamber through a jungle of vivid creepers, snagging underfoot or slung close above you. By dusk the pilgrims have dispersed to their camping grounds, and the place is silent. Now it seems to sag in brilliant ruin, like some game abandoned by children at evening. Its remembered rite carries with it, in spite of everything, a charge of innocent optimism, of earthy piety and trust. In the twilight a few campfires start up around the valley, and a faint perfume lingers: incense lit to feed the unhappy dead, and to please the darkening mountain.

Few beliefs are older than the notion that heaven and earth were once conjoined, and that gods and men moved up and down a celestial ladder – or a rope or vine – and mingled at ease. Some primeval disaster severed this conduit for ever, but it is remembered all through Asia and beyond in the devotion to ritual poles and ladders: the tree by which the Brahmin priest climbs to make sacrifice, the stairs that carry shamans to the sky, even the tent pole of Mongoloid herdsmen, the 'sky pillar' that becomes the focus of their worship. Such cults rise from a vast, archaic hinterland, from the world pillars of early Egypt and Babylon and the ascension mysteries of Mithras, to the heaven-reaching trees of ancient China and Germany, even to Jacob's angel-travelled ladder that ascended from the centre of the world.

These concepts, which spread in part from Mesopotamia, have in common that their life-giving stair or vine, by which sanctity replenishes the earth, exists at the world's heart, the *axus mundi*; and in the sacred pole of Kailas, erected at the heart of the Hindu-Buddhist cosmos, they find a classic exemplar. Its raising was a timeless ceremony – intermittently performed – that marked the Buddha's shallow victory over the Bon, the region's primal faith. For the Bon, Kailas was itself a sky ladder, linking Elysium to earth. The idea of a heaven-connecting rope is old in Tibetan belief, whose first kings descended from the sky by cords of light attached to their heads. By such ropes too it was thought the dead might climb to paradise.

Even in Buddhist myth there is something changing and fragile in the relationship between Kailas and its faithful. For all its mass, the mountain is light. In Tibetan folklore it flew here from another, unknown country – many of Tibet's mountains fly – and was staked in place by prayer banners and chains before devils could pull it underground. Then, to prevent the celestial gods from lifting it up and returning it to where it came from, the Buddha nailed it down with four of his footprints.

But now, they say, it is the age of Kaliyuga, of degeneration, and at any moment the mountain could fly away again.

The mystery of the white-clad figure with a cross is resolved at nightfall. I find him camped among the tents by the Lha river, his monstrous crucifix propped against a lorry. He turns out to be a Russian German, born in Kazakhstan, where Stalin deported his people during the Second World War. He stands gauntly tall, and talks as if delivering a holy ultimatum. Somehow he has blundered here across the complicated borders in his lorry, innocently confident.

I ask in amazement: 'You've had no trouble?'

'Everyone has been good to me. Everyone has welcomed me!' His blue eyes shine cloudless from a gush of ginger hair and beard.

'You're Russian Orthodox?'

'I'm an evangelist.'

His cross is covered with arcane images. A symbol of the world's mouth gapes on the headpiece; at its base a black sheep, signed with skull and crossbones, is pointing hellwards; while in the centre hangs the figure most puzzling to Tibetans: a crucified god.

The evangelist explains these symbols to me in a gruff litany, but I sense in him no expectation of my believing, and I wonder about his journey here, the incomprehension he has suffered. It is more than two centuries since any missionary preached in central Tibet. And now he launches into a credo so jumbled and esoteric that my remembered Russian fails. He has an idea that the people of Atlantis and the world will converge in Christ. 'And the earth's power lines run through the Sphinx – everybody knows this – which faces east towards Kailas, and Kailas . . .'

He goes on and on. His New Age clichés are bathed not only in Jesus but in an old Slavophile dream. The West is mired in materialism, but Russia is pure soul. Russia will be the saviour of the world . . .

'Even now, even under Putin?' I mumble.

'Yes, Putin, Medvedev, they are returning Russia to herself.'

He stands beside his cross, the prophet incarnate, the owner of truth. He craves the world's peace, a perfect ecumenism. If only people would listen. The Buddhists are all right, he says, but they have no Christ. He is bringing them the Russian Christ.

'But they don't understand me. They speak nothing.' It is

his presence alone, with his towering cross, that must beam to others the redemption in his mind. How is his Christian trinity of gods received? I wonder. And God's son, walking in history? But he does not know. The generous Tibetan pantheon, I imagine, might superficially incorporate them. But they, together with the swarm of Buddhas and godlings, must vanish at last like a superstitious mist before nirvana's absolute.

Would he go deeper into China? I ask. But somehow I do not fear for him.

'No. Kailas is my end.' He shakes his head: his hair makes a fiery halo. 'I will be going home now.'

'Where is home?' He is gazing up at the mountain and the charnel ground, and I wonder for a moment if he means to make an end there.

But he says: 'After perestroika my family came westwards, to Germany, where our people started.' So he was returning to the paradigm of Western materialism. 'Düsseldorf,' he murmurs.

CHAPTER FOURTEEN
· · · · · · ·

The true start of the kora is here, on the ridge between the great pole and the river, where the Kangri chorten isolates the mountain in its dark arch. The chorten's base is piled with stones placed by pilgrims before their leaving, and Iswor adds a pebble at dawn, then circles the site clockwise, the prayer beads loosened around his wrist, insuring against danger.

These chortens find their origins far back in the Indian stupas that enshrined the incinerated corpse of the Buddha. But in Tibet they have changed shape and taken other meanings. Some contain funerary remains, but most enfold scriptures and relics, often too damaged to be used but too sacred to destroy. Ours is a ceremonious gateway, purifying the pilgrims' path, and is built on a model now familiar, its square plinth mounting steps to a concave drum that ascends in turn to thirteen dwindling and compacted golden wheels, topped by a crescent moon cradling the sun.

These structures may be seen, predictably, in many ways. Their five chief components, from earthbound base to aerial sun, signify the Buddhist elements, as prayer flags do. But they double as the initiate's path to enlightenment, and a crowning disc on the sun's orb transmutes solar wisdom and lunar compassion into pure truth. Tantric initiates discover in the chorten an eidolon of the seated Buddha, and see its central axis – most chortens enclose a vertical beam – as a symbol of Meru-Kailas, or a male archetype infusing a female body.

We step through the chorten's passage towards a vision of the mountain. Strings of yaks' teeth hang from the ceiling, brushing our shoulders, and two rotting yaks' heads dangle above. Enclosed in the drum above us, invisible relics confer benediction. Then we walk out into the holy valley. Its floor is lacquered green where yaks and *jhaboo*s are grazing. A few pilgrims are strung like beads along it. And here, around the meadows called the Golden Basin, the cliffs start to close magnificently in. Their bluffs break into seams of tangerine and pink, then shiver up like ruined towers to merge with the mountain walls, pouring down shale.

Beside us, hermit caves sprinkle the heights under the charnel ground, where pilgrims are climbing, wild-haired and young. Who had meditated here? Bonchung, perhaps, the early Bon wizard; or Milarepa, the Buddhist saint who dispossessed him? But they do not know. The caves are narrow, with platforms built of loose stones. Worshippers have glued money and prayer beads to the ceilings, and someone has laid her necklace on a stone.

We tramp along an easy path in high spirits. The Lha river wanders alongside, crusted with ice. Kailas looms in solitary snow to the north-east. Along the wide, pebbled valley ahead of us, a figure is inching forward, levelling its length in the dust, rising, advancing three paces, falling again, arms stretched ahead. Even when we draw alongside,

I cannot at first tell if this is a youth or a girl. By these painful means, the body touching every span of the path, a pilgrim may circle the mountain in three weeks, returning each dawn to the spot abandoned, marked with a stone. When the figure rises, I see that it is protected in a leather apron; and the hands, which lift in prayer before each obeisance, are strapped with wooden boards. Out of the dust she turns a blackened face to me, and smiles. If she is initiate, she sees on the path in front her tutelary Buddha, and gathers virtue with every salutation. While two bent women, too old to perform this rite themselves, precede the near-child with a thermos of tea, crouching in the dust before her and willing her on.

Iswor tramps past, as bemused as I, and says only: 'Perhaps she has done something.'

We are entering a zone of such charged sanctity that any penance, or any crime, trembles with heightened force. Its few inhabitants, mostly monks, exist in a force field of intensified holiness, for their past incarnations have led them here. This domain is venerated even beyond Buddhists and Hindus. The surviving Bon worship their ancestral mountain here, circling it anticlockwise, and followers of the peaceful Jain faith – although I cannot identify any – reverence Kailas as the site where their first prophet passed away, and circumambulate it in the Buddhist way, carrying their prayer beads in little bags.

Pilgrims who complete thirteen circuits may walk the inner kora, a short, sometimes dangerous path that approaches the south face. But this is the closest anyone may go. Kailas has never been climbed. At 22,000 feet, it is not a giant by Himalayan standards, but it stands fearsomely solitary. In 1926, a British mountaineer, a Colonel Wilson of the Indian Army, with his sherpa Satan, reconnoitred the southern approaches to the peak, which Wilson likened jauntily to a bowler hat. After toiling up sunless defiles, he thought he identified a ridge that might reach the summit. But time was short. Aghast at the near-perpendicular scarp and the shaly abysses, the two men retreated, while a freak-ish storm of snow and lightning exploded over them.

It was almost twenty years before another British alpinist, Major Blakeney, fancifully imagined scaling the peak armed with little more than an umbrella; but his Tibetan guide adamantly refused. Then, in the mid-1980s, the great moun-taineer Reinhold Messner planned its assault, while the Chi-nese temporised, and the matter petered out. Nobody since then has attempted the summit. The north face is sheer, perhaps unclimbable, and racked by avalanches, the south and west precipitous with shale and glaciers. Only the east, barely visible on the kora, may – or may not – offer a less fearful climb. But the ascent of Kailas is still interdicted above all by a people who will not disturb their gods.

As we go north, these chasms are still out of sight, hidden by intervening cliffs, and even the granite plinth from which the summit rises is barely visible. In this valley where we go – the valley of Amitabha, the Buddha of Infi-nite Light – the sandstone pales to fawn and amber and rushes up near-vertically in friable bluffs. As the valley nar-rows, the advance of the prehistoric glacier that carved out its moraine becomes grimly palpable. Tiny and high against one precipice, the first of the four hermitages that ring the mountain seems little more than a barn, built half-invisibly of the precipice stone. Prayer flags pour from its walls like celestial telegraph to the monstrous gully behind. It was from here, perhaps, that a boulder smashed the monastery five years before Hedin came.

We cross a low bridge downriver and struggle up towards Choku Gompa's walls. The crevices around are pocked with concealed caves, where Padmasambhava hid treasure texts, or Milarepa sat. As we go up, the cliff face across the river rears behind us, indented with seeming castles where a frozen waterfall hangs. Around us the earth is furred with white plants like salinated grass, and there are butter-yellow flowers among the boulders. Far below, the Lha river rushes green, and a train of yaks trickles across the grass-tinged valley floor. A mile away, the ant-like silhouette of Ram is moving north under his double load to a camping site we don't yet know; while to the south a black hyphen seems not to move at all, where the girl pilgrim is inching towards salvation.

Close by, the hermitage might be any age, although a television aerial and satellite dish stick above its roofs. In fact its thirteenth-century predecessor was levelled to the rocks by Red Guards, who destroyed every monastery around the mountain, and every chorten. By the time some Indian pilgrims reached Choku again in 1983, its ruins were attracting legends. It was said to have been vast, sheltering hundreds of travellers at night, and to have housed the arms of the near-mythic Zoravar Singh. In reality the *gompa* had been small and unkempt, like this one. Kawaguchi found it quaintly subject to the ruler of Bhutan, with only four lamas living here.

I discover its monks nested like swallows in little cells whose windows gaze on Kailas. Their lavatory encloses makeshift holes hanging fifty feet above the valley. There are three men only, who speak nothing I understand, and two rumbustious dogs wearing scarlet ruffs, for they too are holy. At the gates of the prayer hall pilgrims are scraping up its dust and stones into pouches. Inside, some 200 candles, each swimming in its cup of oil, draw down a curtain of fiery light. The fumes of yak butter that once reeked through Tibetan shrines have thinned away – replaced by imported plant oil – but the money that pilgrims pay for replenishing the lamps is piled with fruit on the altar. Beyond the pillars the dimming ranks of saints and Buddhas people the shadows with their protection: the Buddhas of Past, Present and Future, the Buddha of Long Life cradling nectar, the Buddha of Wisdom wielding his flaming sword. Here too is the Avalokitesvara of compassion, whose thousand all-seeing arms halo him like a peacock's tail, and the mother goddess Tara, born from his tears, whose great rock crowns the pass ahead tomorrow, the zenith of the pilgrimage, at 18,600 feet.

But the statue most enshrined in pilgrims' awe is barely discernible. Less than quarter lifesize, and so swagged in jewellery that no arm or even neck emerges, the white marble image of the Amitabha Buddha is the oldest and most precious of Kailas. Under its mandarin crown the pale face gazes, emptied of expression. Its eyes seem closed, its smile barely starting. It is said to be 'self-manifest', shaped by its own will from the stone, and to have flown here from its birthplace in the milky waters of an Indian lake. Encased beside it is the white conch shell blown by the saint Naropa a thousand years ago, and near the altar a huge cauldron of chased copper, floating with lights, is the pot where he brewed his tea.

These three relics are treasured as the body, mind and speech of the Buddha. In the seventeenth century the army of the pious king of neighbouring Guge carried them all away, but the statue grew so heavy that it could not be moved from the valley, the conch shell flew into the air, and the cauldron poured out blood, until the army retreated empty-handed. Soon afterwards the statue, lying among rocks, requested of an old man that he return it to Choku, and he carried it back, light as a cloud.

In the turmoil of the Cultural Revolution, the old patronage of Bhutan may have saved the relics, but this is unsure. Already in the nineteenth century a Tibetan pilgrim reported the statue too damaged to assess, and the first cauldron was very likely melted down. In 1991 sixteen artefacts were stolen from the *gompa* for the Western art market; and the conch shell, for all its embossed silver, looks spanking new.

A Tibetan pilgrim, who speaks cautious Mandarin, questions a cheery monk for me. All the relics are old, the monk says, and came here by magic. Sometimes the conch shell is taken to bereaved homes and sounded in the ear of the dead. 'It will light up their way! It will guide them. Sometimes the dead are brought up to the monastery for this.' He speaks with breathy certitude. 'The statue? It is self-made. In former times, it used to speak. It is the Buddha of learning and light. Students with difficulties have come here to learn and recite his mantra . . .'

But when I ask about Kangri Latsen, the monk turns cold. Latsen is the wild, autochthonous god of the heights to which Choku clings, converted to Buddhism, but older and darker, and kept separate, as if secret. But I badger a younger monk with the god's repeated name until he leads me down from the temple terrace through a storeroom and unlocks a door into the near-dark.

At first I can make out nothing. A single butter lamp is burning beneath a drift of white, and a slit window frames Kailas, but sheds no light. The room looks poor as an outhouse, its clay floors cracked. The monk is nervous, girlish. He waits near the door. I discern an altar of plain wood where the white silks hang, and some money thrown beneath. I step up to it. And out of the clouding scarves a red demon's face leers, straggled in red hair. It is glaring at the floor in eerie fixation, its teeth bared and eyes popping and inflamed. Of its body, if it has one, I can see nothing. But it wears a green crown, like a child's paper hat, and dangles a chunky amulet. The altar is flanked by two four-foot elephant tusks, and other faces are grinning from the silks beside it. Buddhists say that these ancient Bon wreckers have been converted to guardians of the faith, but this one seems to exist in angry exile, like a troubling unconscious, and all the gifts bestowed on him to no avail. It was this misanthrope, presumably, who chucked down a boulder on the monastery a century ago.

A group of Khampa pilgrims has crowded in after me, not knowing, I think, what will be here, but fervent to worship. Their women remain outside. The old men buy more scarves to heap beneath Kangri Latsen, beseeching in their gratitude, stooped before the young monk, praying. I watch from the dark in fascinated estrangement, until they file away. Perhaps these raucous local gods – lords of the wind and the avalanche – are easier to comprehend than the otherworldly Buddhas, and more prudent to propitiate on this hardest of all pilgrimages.

The Lha Chu, the River of the Spirits, guides us for five miles more along a corridor of paling sandstone. For 3,000 feet on either side its walls unfurl in towering curtains of pink and copper red. Some softness in the stone pulls it into fissured terraces that cut across the vertical cracks of the cliffs, until the whole rock face splinters to Cyclopean building blocks that travel unbroken for hundreds of yards. Then, high up, torn by wind, the strata thin and grow detached. They ascend to a filigree of turrets and palisades, pierced by the illusion of high-arched doors, until the skyline fills with wrecked palaces and temples. Where the rock turns shell pink, especially, these silhouettes seem to glow in another ether. In between, frozen waterfalls drop out of gullies, or tip over the cliff summits in flashes of ice. When these at last reach the valley at our feet, they melt into tributaries that barely flow, choking the Lha river with splinters.

The mountaintop palaces, of course, are the residencies of Buddha deities, and every oddity of crag or boulder becomes a sign of their habitation, or is the spontaneous self-shaping of some sacred prodigy. In the valley side facing Choku the monks descry sixteen saints clustered in rock, while on the summit floats the silk tent of Kangri Latsen.

Beyond these, as we walk, a mystic stream carries down rainbow light from the mountain, and a rock cupola to the east is the fortress of the Hindu demon Ravana, converted to Buddhism, complete with his yak and his dog. The boulder that projects nearby is the crystal reliquary of the saint Nyo Lhanangpa, enclosing his vision of the Buddha, and beyond this the monkey god Hanuman kneels to offer incense to Kailas. Behind us to the east the tail of the wonderful horse of Gesar of Ling, Tibet's epic king, spills from the heights in an icy cascade, and his seven brothers inhabit seven rock pinnacles along our way. To the west, on three towering 20,000-foot peaks, dwell the three great bodhisattvas of longevity, and a granite boulder beside our track is a serpent-quelling Buddha made manifest. Everywhere, for those with sight, the stone throbs with life. And on Kailas itself gleam the glacial portals to the heart of Demchog's citadel.

In this complex topography Buddhist, Hindu and unregenerate Bon deities and spirits throng the path in overlapping regiments. There are literally thousands of them. Often I can locate a site only by some solitary pilgrim, prostrated where the hand or footprint of a Buddha has burnt like sulphur into the rock. Some of the gods and bodhisattvas fly confusingly between abodes. Others reside in several eyries at once. But always, in some sense, they are corporeal with their petrified dwellings, to which the pilgrim turns to pray. The great lama Gotsampa, searching for hearthstones on which to brew his tea, found none that he could use: for all the stones around him were the self-manifest images of Buddhas, or inscribed with their speech.

Wherever a cave scoops out a cliff and a hermit is remembered, feats of past piety soak into the rock, and the saints continue there in mystic body long after their death. The kora of every pious pilgrim adds its mite to this bank of invisible virtue, and the years-long meditation of a revered saint – Milarepa, Padmasambhava, even the ousted Bonchung – saturates the mountain with its mana. Yet neither devoted ascetics nor conquering Buddha have quite eradicated a suspicion of darker gods. Most of these ancient troublemakers have been converted to meditation deities and protectors like Kangri Latsen, but sometimes their conversion looks shaky, and they backslide. Ranked in tiers up the slopes of Kailas, the *lha* sky gods fight the surrounding *lhamain* (who are destined for hell), and their passions condemn them at last to bitter cycles of rebirth. The common demons that plague Tibetan lives – the *sadak* 'lords of the earth', the black snakes of the *klu* lurking beneath the waters, the terrible armoured *tsen* on their flying red horses – wither to Buddhist servants in the shadow of Kailas, but the mountain's capricious moods – its sudden storms and rock falls – stir countervailing fears and nervous rites of propitiation.

The pilgrims who pass us are few now. They go fast, intent and smiling. Many cover the hard, thirty-two-mile path in thirty-six hours; some will complete it in a single day. And hardship is of the essence. The kora ahead follows an intense trajectory of purification, mounting past sites for the ritual cleansing of sin to the fearsome pass, sacred to Tara, and its climax of redemption. Even these deep-lunged pilgrims may falter in exhaustion on the way. Meanwhile the pulse of the stone footprint under their anointing fingers, of their body prone against the ground, of the gaze of the mountain itself, generate a deep, sensory exchange. You gather empowered earth and pluck healing herbs. You sip divine water. Sin is cleaned like sweat from the body. Your prayers, too, are spoken aloud into the listening air – I hear, but cannot distinguish them – prayers inherited from family maybe, or the mantra murmured like breathing as you go. And at some time you utter the plea that your pilgrimage may aid the enlightenment of all sentient beings.

Behind me in the valley I am startled to see three men walking towards me counterclockwise. I imagine they are Bon, whose older faithful circumambulate this way, against the Buddhist stream, and I tentatively call a greeting. But they pass by with their faces retracted into hoods, averted, as if ashamed, leaving me mystified.

Before the Buddha came, and before Demchog, this was their mountain. Millennia ago, the Bonpo say, their founder Shenrab, sired by a cuckoo, alighted here from heaven, conquered the local demons, and gave the mountain to 360 gods named gekkos, reflecting the lunar cycle of the year. The chief, Gekko, for all his lizardish name, was a terrifying predecessor of Demchog and Shiva, with nine arms and blue-black skin, snorting out blizzards and thunder. His Kailas was a rock-crystal mountain, the earthly emanation of a celestial palace, which would survive the destruction of the world. If the Bonpo's universe was conceived as a tent, Kailas stood as its central pole, piercing the opening that illumined the sun and stars circling within, and the worlds beneath. To the Bonpo this 'Nine-Stacked Swastika

Mountain' is inscribed with the emblem of fortune (rotating anticlockwise) and the footprints of their saints are all about it.

Buddhists contend that Bon is the leftover of a demon-ridden past. But the Bonpo claim that theirs is the primal faith, received from Persia, perhaps, or Central Asia, long before Buddhism. The historical Buddha, they concede, may be an incarnation of their own Shenrab. Their beliefs, in fact, go back to a time when the region around Kailas, the kingdom of Shang-shung, was the first, royal cradle of Tibetan culture. They were priests to the early kings and their practices were rife with sorcery, spirit control and the guidance of the dead. Yogis tower through Bon legends. They hang their clothes on sunbeams and turn into eagles. For at least two centuries this diffused faith fought with an incoming Buddhism and was slowly transformed by it, to re-emerge a thousand years ago as a religion whose tenets were often indistinguishable from the Buddha's.

Buddhism, in turn, imbibed many Bon gods and practices, including sacred dances and prayer flags. And both faiths, it seems, were influenced by the rites and spirits of nameless cults that preceded them. Tibetan Buddhists accept the 'white' Bon uneasily, whose temple statues are yet more savage than theirs, and whose embrace of magic is more wholesale. (The 'black' Bon remain an unmentionable fringe of shamanistic outcasts.) So the interfused faiths co-exist, even in Lhasa's holy of holies. Right up to the Chinese invasion a Buddhist official would depart each year to a shrine near the Yarlung valley, cemetery of Tibet's kings, and there burn butter lamps and scatter grain in a plea to the cuckoo, the holy bird of the Bon, to fly back to Tibet.

He was an old man now, far into his eighties. He sat among cushions in a room high in the Kathmandu monastery he had founded: a simple cell, his bed folded nearby. A monk had placed a tiny cushion on the carpet before him, where I knelt. From the hill opposite, the noises of a Hindu temple – overrun by tourists, mangy monkeys and vermilion-daubed statues – were blurred to rumours in the sultry air.

Nothing in the Rinpoche's face, where the gentle eyes and still-dark eyebrows seemed touched in as afterthoughts, betrayed the long strain of travels fostering Bon communities – he had become a holy figure to them – or his year in a Chinese prison. In 1961 he had tried to escape Tibet with a group of lamas from his monastery, carrying sacred texts and relics.

'Yes, it was very dangerous. Chinese soldiers found us, and many of our blessed ones were killed. I was shot myself . . .' Wounded, he was left for dead. But a nearby family hid him, and he crossed the border to Mustang after twenty-two days, walking by night.

He dismissed all this as long ago. Since then he had outlived his monastery, obliterated by Red Guards, and founded it anew on this green hill in exile. Time was long here. Like the Dalai Lama (who was ten years younger) he meditated alone for hours every day. He looked grounded and content. 'We Bon are older than Buddhism,' he said, 'far older. We go back to the time of shamanism, and nobody knows when that began. And long before Buddhism came to Tibet in the eighth century, these were our texts, our culture . . .'

I forgot, for a moment, that Kailas – once the mountain temple of his faith – had been annexed to Buddhism (there are famous legends reflecting this). Lulled by the Rinpoche's fluent, careful English, by the monastic peace and memory of the mountain, I asked how he perceived its holiness now, and he spoke as he must have taught hundreds in exile, remembering a lost Tibet.

'In the beginning Kailas was just rock – rocks and stones. Without spirit. Then the gods came down with their entourages and settled there. They may not exactly live there now, but they have left their energy, and the place is full of spirits. The best way to describe the gods, I think, is as colonisers. Each one settled his special region, his peaks and ranges, and there his spirits rested after him. And these became places of power.'

No hint of Western rationale, it seemed, inhibited this story. He spoke of gods as he might of urban politics or nomad settlements, with bald certainty. 'Kailas was only ice at first,' he went on, 'then it became a conch shell, pure white, and one day it will be a desert, everything in transition . . . All the same, you know, it is a place for the others. There is a different mountain more sacred to us Bonpo. It is farther to the east, named Mount Bonri. That's where you will find us, yes, circumambulating counterclockwise. Although there is nothing important in this. It is just our custom.'

Often his mouth hung tentatively open, as if it might twist into laughter, and I had the sense that despite his seeming certainties, all for him was fleeting, conditional, and might translate into something else, so that as he spoke on about the divinities, my attention drifted irreverently, wondering if the cuckoo that sired his god Shenrab was *optatus* or *saturatus*, or if the transition of Kailas from glacier to desert was not the future of all our planet.

He had travelled to Kailas himself, he said, long ago. 'I did the kora six times. But it was winter, the wrong time of year. And I was very young. That region of Shang-shung is very cold, and we walked on compacted snow. It is not my Tibet.' He asked suddenly: 'Was it green when you were there? Was there any spring?'

'Yes, in the valleys.'

He was smiling. He wanted to remember his country in flower. He said: 'Perhaps you love those mountains, but I do not. I come from another region, from the east. It was always green there.' For a little while, before he retired to meditate, he became a homesick old man, remembering, enquiring. Had I been east of Lhasa? Had I been to Kham? Seated in the humidity of Kathmandu, he wanted to hear of the green yak pastures of his home, of the horses grazing, and the waterfalls unfreezing on the high hills.

The pink walls of the Amitabha valley, which have steered Iswor and me ever closer to Kailas, now break stupendously apart, and all at once, barging out from behind separating crags, the mountain hangs above us, close and violent. The smooth dome has gone, and the whole western face is slung into massive eaves of black rock, tiered one upon the next like a gigantic pagoda. Its curving overhangs descend concentrically to glacial ledges that shelter basins of pure snow, while above the white fields banked on its summit flies a wind-driven dust of silver.

It is only noon, but the people have thinned away. I do not at first understand this. Often I see nothing ahead in the wide, turning valley but the solitary speck of Iswor, as it was in Nepal, and some Austrian trekkers strung out on the trail. Where have the pilgrims gone?

But others are approaching now, moving counterclockwise, many astride ponies or yaks. As they draw near, I see that they are not Bon, but Indian Hindus, turning back. They straggle in a sad army. Their Tibetan drovers whistle and shout alongside, but the pilgrims ride in silence, hooded and swathed, their faces in shadow. They do not speak as they pass. Many look utterly spent, the men's faces like dark ash, frosted in moustaches, their eyes lowered. Some of them clutch canisters of oxygen, which they will jettison, when empty, among the rocks. For an hour or two there seems nothing on the mountain but a few blond trekkers muscling forward and this train of dark pilgrims descending.

The wind has turned to cutting ice, blowing from Kailas. The mountains ahead show bare flanks or broken scripts of snow. A figure descends alone, bulked in a brown anorak and balaclava, stopping to zip her hood under her eyes. Her party comes from Bangalore, she says, in India's far south, and nothing prepared them for this. Her voice is light and gutted in the wind.

'I don't know what happened to us. Our people were so sure they could do it. We went through government tests for our health – lungs, heart, everything. Maybe some of our group avoided them, I'm not sure.' She sounds less tired than stunned. Of her face, encased by hood and dark glasses, I can see nothing but wisps of escaped hair, greying, and the scarlet *tika* outlined black on her forehead, which looks somehow tragic. 'We numbered sixty-eight when we started, but half of us turned back at Lake Manasarovar because of health – poor chests, coughing blood. Two of us died there, one a woman of just forty. Something happened in her breast. So we began to feel afraid. We are not used to this cold. I suppose you in the West are used. I am full of sadness now. The rest of us went on and got up to seventeen thousand feet, and then we couldn't climb further. Our nerve was broken. That is why we turned back before finishing our *parikrama*. I am very sad now, and rather ashamed.'

Behind her the last of her party is passing down the ravine. A woman in flowery pantaloons sits half fainting on a horse led by a fierce herdsman, her husband walking alongside, trying to hold her.

The woman beside me takes off her dark glasses from alert, rather beautiful eyes. She says: 'All the same, Lake Manasarovar was wonderful. We all waded in a little and washed its water over us, from the head down and – do you know? – we never felt it cold, but quite warm, because of its sanctity.' She smiles to herself. 'At least we had that.' Then she resumes the long descent of the valley, wrapping her arms around herself, not looking back.

I walk on with vague foreboding, listening to my body. Hindu pilgrims seem to have reached Kailas pitifully ill-prepared ever since ragged Shaivite renunciates straggled here in the nineteenth century, begging. In the 1930s the pilgrim numbers mushroomed, and every year several thousand caste Hindus were attempting the *parikrama*, their kora. Long after the hiatus of the Cultural Revolution, in 1981, a few hundred pilgrims, chosen by Indian government lottery, moved over the Lipu Lekh pass west of Nepal. These sponsored pilgrims now number a thousand a year – a fraction of those who enter the lottery – but other tour operators ignore official precautions. Health stipulations are routinely flouted. The pilgrims are often middle-aged business people, modestly pious. I had seen them crowded into dormitories in Taklakot. Many are from the south, from lowland cities like Bangalore and Chennai: devotees of Shiva. Yet often they are flown from Kathmandu to Lhasa, ascending almost 8,000 feet in an hour, then truck four days west to reach Manasarovar exhausted at 15,000 feet. In the past few days, eight have died on the mountain.

The valley is edging up more steeply now, the wind intensifying. The black-white scarps of Kailas glitter cruelly close. Mountains in many cultures have been coterminous with death. In Indian myth, Yama, the first man to die, climbed a mountain over 'the high passes', showing the way. High above me, released by some melted snow shelf, an ice-bound stream crackles into life and runs glittering down the cliff. I wonder what it means to die here. Some Buddhists say that merit is annulled if the kora is not complete, as if the anticlockwise descent were a slipping back in time. Yet perhaps the Hindu party, touched by the lake waters, feel purified. The track ahead of me is empty of anyone to ask. But as the last pilgrim drops from sight under the gleam of

Kailas, the beliefs of many peoples – from ancient Egypt to aboriginal Australia – seem starkly natural. The mountain path is the road of the dead. The Assyrian word for 'to die' was 'to clutch the mountain'. Many Altaic peoples imagine their souls departing up a mystic range. And in Japan, the traditional funeral cortége still departs with the cry: '*Yamaguki!* We go to the mountain!'

As the track bends north-east, the ethereal sandstone disappears. The slopes turn black with granite, and the mountain's lower ridges break into unstable spikes and revetments. Their ribs are slashed in chiaroscuro, and their last outcrops pour towards the valley in the fluid, anthropomorphic shapes that pilgrims love. The spine and haunches of a massive stone beast, gazing at Kailas, are hailed as the Nandi bull, holy to Shiva; another rock has become the votive cake of Padmasambhava.

To the west, beneath the last black and orange cliffs of the Amitabha basin, the second *chaksal gang* prostration platform spreads under wind-torn flags, where the Buddha nailed Kailas to earth with a footprint that still indents the stone. Soon afterwards the trail is trickling through the meadows of Damding Donkhang, and nomad tents are pitched along the stream. Gradually the way starts bending east. A frozen tributary departs up the Wild Yak Valley, leaving the Lha contracted almost to pure ice. Now the mountain's western face is revolving away from us, and we glimpse another face more awesome and absolute, softened for a while by the intervening crag of Vajrapari. Within an hour Iswor and I – he tired beneath his double load, uncomplaining – are clambering up to Drira Phuk Gompa, the Monastery of the Cave of the Yak Horns. Small and rough-stoned as the others, it is locked against the desolate valleyside among huge boulders, facing the mountain.

Halfway up Iswor turns with a quaint thumbs-up sign and cries out: 'Are you happy?'

I answer, not knowing: 'Yes! Are you?' But I am somehow uneasy.

'If you are happy, I am happy!'

A boy-monk hurries us in, and the harshening wind drives us from the courtyard and the flag-streaming terraces. We cannot stay here. The pilgrims' rooms are full, although we see nobody, and Ram has pitched our tent still higher up against the snows, where we will acclimatise near 17,000 feet and try to sleep.

In the temple the familiar skylight, fringed with tankas, is darkening towards evening. The altar is crowded with miniature stupas in barley or buckwheat, some painted, left by pilgrims who have gone. The tables blaze with artificial flowers, and tiers of scalloped niches hedge the walls in faded yellow and gold. Here, banked in their toy-like casements, the divinities sit in near-darkness. I glimpse their Olympian smiles and hands hovering in blessing, the fall of necklaces. Their folded legs and torsos glimmer gold. Each niche is fringed with pilgrims' money.

Drira Phuk was once the richest of the little monasteries round Kailas. Kawaguchi found that it housed several senior lamas, and in 1935 the scholar Giuseppe Tucci came upon a woodblock printing press here, from which the monks copied out a rare pilgrim's guide for him. Now I find its monks curled among cushions, warmed by a yak-dung oven. Iswor tries to talk with them in Tamang, and I in Mandarin, but they speak neither. Two of them doze while another – an eerily beautiful youth with long locks and girl's hands – brings us tea with salt and yak butter, then falls asleep.

Their monastery, in its strange way, commemorates the kora itself. In the thirteenth century the sage Gotsampa was the first to circumambulate the mountain, lured along this valley by a *dri*, a female yak. He followed her into the cave above us, and found the imprint of her horn on the rock where she had vanished. She was, he realised, a *dakini* in disguise, a fairy sky-dancer named Senge Dongpa. As he settled in the cave to meditate, she returned to minister to him, and thereafter generations of Kagyupa hermits settled here. So he became the founder of the kora.

Now the only monk awake, an eager acolyte with hedge-hog hair, takes us deeper into the rock face by a passage bright with painted bodhisattvas. They gaze from blue-washed casements and float in fresco across the walls. The cave is a slanted overhang of living rock, where the saint's seat has smoothed to an altar. Under the monk's guiding hand, I feel in its ceiling the long, tapering groove where the *dri*'s horn parted the cliff. A gilded statuette of Gotsampa still meditates here, barely visible in the glow of a lone lamp. I crouch before it. The monk points to a figure encased nearby. 'Senge Dongpa!'

I stare at her in amazement. The *dakini* is not the fairy seductress I had imagined, but a demon goddess with a pig's face and lewd fangs, waving a sword. She has transformed into the

Lion-faced Celestial Angel of this upper valley, as fluid as her rocks. As I turn away, an old pilgrim stoops beside us with a gift of butter to replenish the lamp, and asks – Iswor says – that he be remembered in the monk's prayers in this place of power.

Before we leave, Iswor, suddenly nervous, wants to pray to the goddess Tara, who owns the 18,600-foot pass that we must scale tomorrow. In the chief shrine her white body is so garlanded in jewellery that even the eyes that open on her hands and feet are blinded. But a third eye gazes from her golden forehead in a face of vapid sweetness, and the blue lotus of compassion floats behind her. Other pilgrims have sought assurance too, and the fingers of her right hand, raised in mercy, are so clotted with votive money that their gesture is lost. Iswor places two lamps at her foot, bows and whispers to me: 'Light one for your future.' Then he finds his ponderous backpack again, and we go out into the rasping cold.

From here as we descend through the twilight, the north face of Kailas breaks on the dimming sky. Two closer mountains – the pyramids of Vajrapani and Avalokitesvara, the peaks of power and benevolence – frame it like twin sentinels. Tantric adepts, inspired by the mountains' symmetry, are enjoined to celebrate this moment in the mandala of Supreme Bliss, where Hindus envisage Shiva and Buddhists whatever deity is guiding their salvation. Beyond, a third pyramid mountain, sacred to Manjushri, the destroyer of ignorance, completes a triad to symbolise the attributes of the Buddha, while still farther east, beyond our narrowing path tomorrow, there hangs the pass of the compassionate Tara, to whom we lit our feeble lamps.

As we turn closer against the mountain, the Lha valley

disappears northwards, towards the source of the Indus, and we are climbing steep up the dark moraine of a tributary. Beside us, as if by the revolution of a giant wheel, the mountain's western face, with its vast hammocks of snow ledge, has followed the smooth beauty of the southern face out of sight, and into their place has risen this curtain of sheer terror. For the first time the whole mountain is exposed above us. From crest to foot it falls 5,000 feet in a near-vertical precipice. Nothing softens its chill descent. Its scarp is jet black, barely seamed with ice. Near its crest the snow plummets for hundreds of feet in razor sheets, and white pendants like inverted fans overlap one another six or eight high, descending in ghostly tiers to the abyss.

Trembling in my hands, the only guide to the mountain likens this face to the 'north wall of the Eiger from Grindelwald'. Perhaps it is a submerged memory of this mountain that has chilled me for long minutes. Grindelwald was where my sister died, killed by an avalanche at the age of twenty-one. Between rock and snow, skiing. In the shadow of the Eiger. My lungs feel lined with cold. Ancient glaciers have scoured the ravines around into granite walls. For years my stricken mother could not speak of her, her memory under silence. We are climbing into near-darkness. The temperature has dropped far below freezing. I am shivering as if my padded anorak and thermal layers are muslin. Buddhists discern on the north scarp of Kailas a devil leading a pig, and the palace of a serpent king. But I have stopped looking.

My father is at the police station, I in the hotel lobby, where my mother asks some strangers to pray for us. It is only now that I feel afraid. My mother never importuned anyone. We sink our faces in our hands, waiting. For an hour, perhaps, or a minute, there is no news from the mountain. Then the door opens on my father, who says: 'It's no good . . . no good.' He folds my mother in his arms.

It is years before her smile straightens, or I travel among mountains.

Our tent is pitched against a narrow ledge, anchored by boulders. A night wind comes scything up the valley. We bolt down noodles and warm tuna, then ease into our sleeping bags, fully dressed. Ram is quiet, tired, and Iswor's head is throbbing with the first signs of altitude sickness. I can give him only aspirin. Tomorrow we will be climbing another 1,600 feet within three hours, and I wonder when the first nausea may hit us all. I try to sleep, but instead I lie febrile and clear-headed, listening for Iswor's sound. Breathing is shallower at night, and the pain intensifies. But I hear nothing, and in this impoverished air my thoughts veer into delirium. All night the wind sets the tent flaps slapping against my head. I imagine I hear voices outside, and clouds rolling over the mountains.

CHAPTER FIFTEEN

· · · · · · ·

Before dawn, when I emerge from our tent, the sky is still ablaze with stars, the wind has vanished, and the silence is the utter, pristine silence of a great desert. But we are more than 17,000 feet high. The air seems so thin that my voice would shatter it. Even my breathing, deeper than usual, sounds too loud, so that I sit down on a rock to quieten it, and wait for the faint white light to seep into the valley below.

Iswor wakes with his headache gone, sturdy and confident again. Ram cooks up three fried eggs – a luxury – and dismantles the tent around us. The coffee goes cold as we drink it. My head is light, not quite mine, but my body shakes off any aches, and a visceral excitement muffles the alarm of the high pass ahead. We set out into the pallor of an invisible sun, risen far below our horizon. We have fourteen miles to go before dark.

The basin where we climb is still deep in snow, covering the frozen Drolma-la river. A sunken bridge lies wrecked in its prison of ice. In front of us, as we gingerly cross the snowfield, the mountains north of Kailas come to the valley in flying buttresses. Behind, the massifs beyond the Lha Chu are powdered in the first morning cloud. The cold is bitter.

Under our feet we hear the wakened river echoing in its ice tunnels, descending unseen.

After a while a moraine named the Valley of Incense opens to our south. A ridge like the section of a vast amphitheatre closes it off, lifting in a long spine to the summit of Kailas, which has transformed again, half-hidden in ashen cloud.

Yesterday I wondered why the pilgrims seemed so few, but now I realise. Many start long before dawn, and complete the kora in less than two days. Sometimes they camp among the rocks. And already by early morning other pilgrims are coming up the snow valley behind me. They climb in scattered groups of two or three, old people marching with sticks and prayer wheels, nomads driving laden yaks. They go in a motley of novelty and tradition, some in long coats that sag open at the throat and bulk above sashed waists, others in peaked caps and quilted jackets. They look unquenchably happy. Sometimes they greet me as they pass, as if their faith was mine. They tramp over these stones in cheap trainers and slipper-thin shoes. Makeshift bundles hang across their shoulders on fraying rope. You marvel at their speed, their delight: they, who have suffered the dislocation of everything they value. The old, especially. You think of the Cultural Revolution, the Chinese war on faith, and you wonder what they have suffered, what inflicted. But their smiles, when they break, seem those of children. Among the women a slash of vivid apron may show, or a glint of smothered jewellery. Some carry babies on their backs – inert under bobble hats – or shepherd children tenderly beside them.

What they are seeing, I cannot tell. Some murmur their *Om mani padme hum* like an urgent pulse, and the prayer beads tremble through their fingers. Most go undeviating, as if the kora contains its own meaning, beyond articulation. Buddhist lore claims that if the eyes are purified, the land transforms. In a small gap between stones – so runs a sacred guidebook – the high lama may perceive a great city, a lesser yogi a fine hut, and the ordinary eye a patch of rock and scrub. A perfect adept might gaze up at Kailas and discern the palace of Demchog with sixteen attendant goddess mountains, but he transfigures this view inwardly to a mandala peopled by bodhisattvas, the goddesses multiply to sixty-two, and he is guided to other knowledge as if layers of illusion have peeled away.

But little of this touches the pilgrims overtaking me. Their world is close at hand, more sensory. The earth under their feet may yield medicinal herbs. The self-shaped stones are obviously gods, or at least sites of divine indwelling. Kailas may be a king, and its foothills his ministers. And a horde of lesser spirits besiege the pilgrim's way. Sky-dancers and mountain godlings are only just out of sight.

Knowledge of these half-seen inhabitants – their where-abouts and power – was codified in pilgrim guidebooks as early as the thirteenth century. A few are still in use. Their narratives have trickled down orally from educated pilgrims to illiterate ones, who seal them with reported miracles. These are the Baedekers of the pious. They lay a tracing paper over the physical landscape, transforming it with stories, ordering it into sanctity. So Kailas becomes symmetrical. It deploys four prostration sites, and its humble *gompas* are seen as shining temples at its cardinal points. Their statues and treasures are reverently inventoried. Every peak and hummock now assumes a Buddhist title. Meditation caves overflow with the visions of named ascetics, even to within living memory. Any abnormality of cliff or boulder – a chance stain, a weird hollow – is identified with the passage of a saint, or the deed of a local hero. And this terrestrial path to merit may be buttressed by mundane directions for reaching one site from another, including calculated times of travel and the matter-of-fact assessment of virtue that will accrue.

The fullest pilgrim guide to Kailas was composed by a Kagyu monk over a century ago. He listened to oral traditions and copied earlier texts. No pilgrim can visit half the sites he names. His early chapters describe the creation of the world from assembled winds and rain, then move on to the inchoate battles of spirits and demons, and the conversion of Kailas's gods to Buddhism. The author mentions another authority who claims that Demchog does not reside on Kailas. This he piously refutes. Then follows a step-by-step guide packed with marvels in the practical language of long-established truth. In a single, short side-alley ahead of us, the footprint of a tantric master mingles with those of five sky-dancer families, and a self-created image of Demchog's consort is followed by one of a wrathful protector. Then comes the petrified nipple of a demoness and a cave sacred to Avalokitesvara, which will cure leprosy, and at last the footprints in stone of Kagyupa lamas, to which the author somehow adds his own. Finally he warns: 'As for my assertions that "This is a deity, and this is its palace," it is inappropriate to hold heretical views which consider these to be exaggerated merely for the reason that they are invisible to ordinary perception.'

As we ascend, the Drolma-la river clatters the other way, broken from its ice shell; the valleysides heap up with fractured granite and the unseen spirits are saluted by multiplying cairns and rock-carved mantras. Diverging to our south, an ill-defined track called the Secret Path of the Dakinis, forbidden to common pilgrims, follows a streamlet between mountains. Its way is higher and shorter than ours, rejoining it five miles farther; but few dare travel it. The sky-dancers are both benign fairies and mountain protectors. Their knowledge is ancient, probably pre-Buddhist. They grant the power to fly or pass through rock, and teach the language of birds. But they may suddenly take hideous forms, like the porcine muse that had shocked me at Drira Phuk, and they may go on to wreak death.

Beyond their path, where Kailas hangs clouded and other mountains start to barge in, our way levels out along the river bank, and we are suddenly tramping through a rubbish tip. Iced and rotted clothes lie snarled in a sprawling mound, or strewn over the surrounding rocks. But their disorder is not random. The bleached garments, even the sloughed shoes, were mostly laid here whole and almost new. There are bags, boots, socks, hats. For a hundred yards up the nearby slope the boulders are clothed with pullovers and caps. One wears a necklace, another a new silk scarf. Yet another is glued with a tuft of human hair.

We are walking across the Vajra Yogini burial ground, which Indians, remembering a holy cremation site back home, call Shiva Tsal. The plateau above was once a sky burial place. The cairns that cover it appease the restless *dakini* whose charnel ground this is, and the corpses of those who die unknown on pilgrimage are sometimes dumped here, their merit assured. Iswor, whose faith is routine, circles the cloth heap sombrely, and climbs on ahead. I wait, catching my breath, sheltering from the risen wind, which is dragging faded garments across the stones.

This cemetery, for all its squalid aspect, is for many the heart of their kora. What is buried here is not physical corpses, but the flotsam of past lives. The shedding of clothes or hair is an offering to Yama, the god of death, that he may ease the wanderings of the dead through limbo towards their next incarnation. Pilgrims may even leave a tooth or shed some drops of blood as a surety that they be remembered when they die. I watch them pass in desultory groups. A man pauses to raise a little pile of stones, and places something beneath. A family of shepherds circumambulate the clothes, emitting faint cries, to the *dakinis* perhaps, or to one another. Their hair straggles under wide-brimmed hats, or flies in shaggy haloes. Their dog rolls among the clothes. A party of Japanese Buddhists photographs the place, mystified.

Later a young man walks up towards the plateau and places a garment there. He speaks cautious English, but cannot quite explain. 'You put something precious to you. You put something close to you.' He splays his hand. 'Some people cut off nails from their fingers. I've just put my favourite shorts up there.'

I ask gently: 'Why?'

He pauses. The question is somehow wrong. This is simply what you do. At last he points at the sky. 'Because you will go upwards!'

I see him climbing fast along the path, where Indians are labouring up on horseback into the wind.

The meanings of this site multiply. Some pilgrims deposit a garment of their beloved dead, even a photograph or a pinch of funerary ash, and pray for them in whatever incarnation they survive. Yet the Buddhist living cannot help the deceased, whose souls do not exist. Such hopes fly in the face of karmic law, and flower through some inchoate instinct, comforting the mourner, not the mourned. For nothing cherished or even recognisable endures. In this cold, weakened air I stare a little wretched at the heap of rags, which seems to symbolise pure loss: the loss that mourns the tang of all human difference, of a herdsman's impromptu song, perhaps, the lilt of a laugh in Grindelwald, or the fingers that caress a favourite dog. On the slopes beside me the dressed-up rocks, plucked by the wind, look like dwarfs watching.

A few yards away a bundle of clothes rises to its feet. An old man has been lying there, with closed eyes. His sash is askew, and the sheepskin lining trickles from his sleeves. Here people practise their own death. Sometimes a whole party will lie prostrate, overseen by a lama. But now there is only this old man, who grins at me and walks on. A little way above us, beneath the grim peak of Sharmari, a russet slab of rock named 'the Mirror of the King of Death' reflects back to the pilgrims all their past sins. Some call this a vision of hell. Armed with its warning, and with the ritual shedding of their dress, their past life, they continue upwards. This is the heart of the kora. Here it quickens into a more intense trajectory. The pilgrim has passed into ritual death. Both Hindus and Buddhists enter this state. They have a thousand feet more to climb. Their breathless ascent to the pass of Tara will release them to new life.

So we climb through the landscape of temporary death. The valley steepens around us, and its fractured granite, sometimes milky or coral, litters the floor in darkening chunks. The river rustles alongside, and a new massif is filling the horizon in parapets of rock and gullied snow.

In its shadow the pilgrims wend like ants to their mountain salvation. They are mostly poor, and the mindfulness of death may rarely be far. The passage between one incarnation and another – the journey they are enacting now – is old in their faith. The first and last teachings of the Buddha himself dwelt on impermanence, and Tibetan funerary rites are steeped in the Book of the Dead. This is their sole text familiar to the outer world. I read it in youth, and even after returning to it, disenchanted, it has touched my journey like the light of a dead star.

For its Great Liberation by Hearing charts the most stupendous voyage of all, through the country of death and resurrection. Its words are spoken aloud into the ear of the corpse, to comfort and guide it to a higher incarnation. Ideally uttered by a pious lama, this scripture brings directions from the enlightened living to the perplexed spirit. It sounds with a disturbing, hypnotic force. The reality of what it envisions – the Buddhas and deities encountered on the journey of the dead – sounds with the magisterial certainty of a voice so insistent and clinically exact that its prescriptions attain the force of proven truth. This blend of spiritual omnipotence and scientific precision has lent it a peculiar allure for the West. Jung called the book his constant companion, and floated the fancy that these ancient lamas might have twitched the veil from the greatest mystery of all. It fascinated the counterculture of R.D. Laing and William Burroughs, and in the mid-sixties Timothy Leary proposed its rite as a psychodrama fuelled by LSD.

In Tibet itself, where it forms a practical funeral rite, the Great Liberation is favoured above all by the old sects of Nyingma and Kagyu, and by the Bon. It rests on the belief that for forty-nine days after the breath has gone, the dead are not quite dead, and that instruction given to the corpse (or beside its bed or usual seat) can still be heard and acted on. For three days the dead experience a pure white radiance, which fills them with fear and bewilderment. But in their ear, out of the mortal world, sounds the voice of the Liberation: *O Child of Buddha-Nature, listen! Pure inner radiance, reality itself, is now coming before you . . .*

In death, an advanced yogi recognises this light as that of pure emptiness – it is sometimes described as transparent moonlight – and passes into nirvana. Then the sound of sacred instruments may be heard, and rainbows appear.

But for most others, as the light fades, a series of benign Buddhas arises, blazingly illumined, and continues for seven days. Each is accompanied by the dull, sensuous light of the once-experienced world, and the words half-chanted to the dead urge the spirit not to flinch, but to recognise and meld with Buddhahood. Each time the spirit slips back into worldly illusion, another Buddha arises, and the guiding voice of the Liberation tenderly repeats itself: *O Child of Buddha-Nature, that which is called death has now arrived. You are leaving this world. But in this you are not alone. This happens to everyone* . . .

Only after these first invocations fail do the visions fade and others more horrible surface. Over renewed cycles of seven days, wrathful deities stampede through the brain, monsters jewelled in snakes and bones. Their entwined consorts offer no comfort: they feed them skullfuls of blood. Yet even now, if these are recognised as aspects of devotional gods, and finally as emanations of the self, the spirit of the dead may liberate itself into the realm of the bodhisattvas.

O Child of Buddha-Nature, now you have wandered to here . . . Where such visions arise, do not be afraid or terrified. Your body is a mental body, formed of habitual tendencies. Therefore, even if you are slain and cut in pieces, you will not die.

But if the spirit does not dispel these ghosts, it becomes mired still deeper in delusion. The terror induced by its past deeds intensifies. The blood-drinking deities become one with Yama, the Lord of Death, whose mirror is even now reflecting the sins of the pilgrims toiling round Kailas towards the pass of compassion. The astral body of the dead can move anywhere at will, but its wretchedness only increases. It returns to its old home, but cannot re-enter its body, even if this still exists. It hears its family mourning, but they cannot hear it calling back. Now its past actions mass like a hurricane behind it. One by one, as the nightmare gods gain credence, they grow more terrifying. The spirit flees into darkness, hears mountains crumble, tries to squeeze into crevices. At last Yama weighs its sins and virtues as black and white pebbles, then beheads and dismembers the undying spirit, which still does not recognise that even this is illusion.

O Child of Buddha-Nature, listen . . . If you continue to be distracted, the lifeline of compassion , suspended to you, will be cast off and you will move on to a place where there is no prospect of liberation. So be careful . . .

Hereafter the dead are condemned to reincarnation. Six 'womb entrances' confront them, leading to the regions of the mortal gods and antigods, of reborn humans, animals, ghosts and the final zone of hell. The spirit starts to recognise the kind among whom it belongs. Yet even now there are prayers and practices for blocking one womb and entering another. At the funeral's end the presiding lama manipulates a placard inscribed with the name of the dead, stopping up wombs and reconciling sins until the spirit has found its place.

The monk Tashi, back in Kathmandu, told me how he spoke this Liberation above the corpse of his grandfather. 'He was a lama, a man who had done good in the village,' he said. 'He can't have suffered much. All the same, in this intermediate state, the soul may not know it is dead. It can see all these mourners crowded round something, weeping. But it may take a long time to realise, as it wanders.'

In the monastery garden, in the blaze of scentless hibiscus and marigolds, this voyage seemed unimaginably remote. But Tashi spoke with the same unshakeable authority as his scripture. 'The soul may put its foot in a stream, perhaps, then notice that no foot is there; or it may suddenly see that its body casts no shadow. Then it realises that it is dead . . .'

Tashi attributed the Book of the Dead to Padmasamb-hava. But in fact its rite seems to have been compiled from fourteenth-century sources, and standardised 300 years later by a feared mystic named Rikzin Nyima Drakpa, who performed dubious miracles on Mount Kailas.

In its duel between ignorance and realisation, illusion and the light of emptiness, this infernal journey seems to gather to itself an unnerving cosmic coherence. There were even those, the *delok*, who had returned from the dead, Tashi warned me (they were mostly women, it seemed) with blissful or hair-raising messages.

I had heard of these people, I said, and they seemed to bring back reflections only of their own culture. Had anyone ever returned with something startlingly different?

Tashi seemed then to become credulous, childlike, and talked of incidents in which people had recognised their past in others. 'I heard about a little girl in a village in our area, reincarnated from a dead child in the village next door. Suddenly she ran into the home of her earlier birth, calling out her old parents' names. Nobody could explain it . . .'

'But in your faith, can the knowledge of a previous life exist?' I heard my own voice unsteady. For the Buddhist soul did not recognise its past. It transmuted continually into another body, another childhood, other parents. 'Isn't every-thing shed?' I sounded harsh, I knew, because I wanted it otherwise. What anxiety could it be that expected this humble monk to hold life's secrets?

He smiled, as he tended to do at contradiction. 'That is so. Only karma lasts. Merit and demerit.'

'So nothing of the individual survives.' Nothing that retains memory?'

'No.' He sensed the strain in me, said with faint regret: 'You know our Buddhist saying?'

Yes, I remember.

From all that he loves, man must part.

Kailas is slipping away. The twin crags of Sharmari are pushing into its place, and its summit has transformed again. From here, with half its northern face occluded by other ranges, it no longer resembles the Eiger at Grindelwald or any mountain I remember. Its dome is light with travelling cloud. Its pendant fans look pretty, like dunces' hats or hanging bells. The starved air hangs still.

Trekkers at high altitudes sometimes sense a person walking a few paces behind them, just out of sight. Often this person is dead. I never feel this, but once or twice I imagine someone walking a little ahead of me.

I am only nineteen and I am mourning, selfishly, the person you would have been for me. For a while your voice is playful beside me. We are approaching 18,000 feet. Am I all right? Day-dreaming brother. No sense of responsibility. Yes, I am all right.

For a long time I have lost the person I was with you. And I reimagined your face so often that the images overlie you.

The track is steepening. The yaks and *jhaboos* that had been following the stream bed are lumbering among the pilgrims now. Often I stop against a boulder, gasping for breath, fearing the first spasm of altitude sickness, which does not come. Ahead stretches a long stadium of mountains whose rocks show black against a thickening carpet of snow. All colour has been wrung out of it. Only the sky shines intermittent blue above the flow of ridges into the valley. In this icy air the people are so swathed and goggled that among the fast-moving Tibetans, swinging their strings of prayer beads, their staffs, their thermoses of buttered tea, it is hard to tell Indian from German, Austrian, even a pair of Russians. A herdsman has brought his two mastiffs with him, collared in red wool, for their merit.

The boulders become teeming sites of veneration. We walk through a broken labyrinth of granite: rocks the size of cottages, powder grey, shell pink. Milarepa defeated his Bon rival here by stacking a third giant boulder on to the wizard's second one, and left behind this toppling pillar, stamped with his footprints.

To the pilgrims there are no mute stones. They disperse and sit familiarly among them. There are boulders that they squeeze between to test their virtue, another that they crawl beneath. The rocks become the judgement of the mountain. One outcrop, named the Place of Black and White Sins, forms a crude tunnel through whose symbolic hell the pilgrim must crush himself before returning down another passage to a higher state. In such crevices the living stone senses the purity of any body passing through, and may contract so violently that the guilty are half entombed.

Three pilgrims, sitting pleasantly together, remember a time when the twin rocks facing them came to judgement.

They speak to Iswor haltingly in Tamang, but they cannot enter the rock passage. It looks impassably narrow, and is blocked solid by ice. The thinnest person may be trapped here, they say. The rock knows everything. Two years ago they levered a fat friend through. 'He was as tall as you!' they cry at me, and disintegrate into helpless merriment. One of them pushed, two of them pulled, and after half an hour, they say, the man emerged thinner, sinless but bloodied and half suffocated. Could I not wait for the ice to melt?

But the track carries us up again, and the mountain valley closes unsoftened around our strange, heterogeneous trickle of beasts and humans drawn up like iron filings to the pass. We go through intermittent sunlight. Whenever it clouds, the air freezes round us. The crust of snow, printed with yaks' hooves, is crisp and hard underfoot, even in June. A sharp wind has risen. Far ahead of us, the path elongates along the hillsides, until its pilgrims become snow and granite. We are climbing through a monochrome limbo. Hundreds of cairns and inscribed rocks litter the track and bristle on the skylines. Among their boulders the scarlet scarves of women flicker and disappear again. I am barely an hour from the summit. Somewhere to our right the Drolma river has died away. Impassive trains of yaks, some with blond heads and tails, are marching up behind me, their cloven hooves smiting the rocks, and their riders – anxious Hindus – clinging to padded saddles. And once a whiskered ancient in threadbare trainers, overtaking me at ease, clasps my shoulder in a shaking hand that kindles a shock of warmth.

We come to a sacred rivulet where yaks are drinking.

Its tributary is sought above all by butchers, who here wash away the sin of killing animals. Iswor has stopped too, so swathed in scarves that he shows only a pair of watchful eyes. He says: 'We can't stay long at this height. My head . . .'

Another man is walking behind me: a pilgrim, with his wife and child and beast. Recent centuries have not touched him. He has his own. He sees with a bright, focused intensity. He has come from lake country to the north, or perhaps from farther, and the distance brings merit. He prostrates often to the god mountain, and the earth feels hot under him. The prayer's words are strong, although he does not understand them, and the gods breathe back from the summits. He has remembered everything the village shaman spoke of, and placated the *klu* in the stream, in case they are there. The water's coldness comes cleansing to the touch. He puts it in a phial for his sick mother. That is what he has come for, and for the black earth-lords to spare his barley crop, and for the calving of the third yak. These are the great things. His wife, whom he shares with his brother, has other thoughts. Women's. He knows what they are, he thinks.

In the last monastery he burnt rhododendron leaves and a juniper twig while the god's eyes watched him in the lamplight: Chenresig, the many-armed (was that he?). He had offered enough *tsampa* to alert the god's attention, he was sure. And lit a butter lamp. Then he had asked that the Chinese leave Tibet; they had taken his grandfather to a camp somewhere, and returned him dead. He remembers his father crying. There was the Great Elephant Cave too, full of hermits' feats, where he poured out some *chang* from his thermos. The monk gave him a pill baked from holy clay, which cost a little. At the cemetery he snipped a woollen patch from his *chuba*, and left it there. He felt lighter after this. His wife left a bead. So the god of death might spare them worse futures. They are clean now.

Our path swerves up through glacial debris to the last ascent. The hills beneath us look rough-skinned, half-created. Their only colours are those we bring, and a sudden, copper-red stain of lichen over the boulders. My head is free of pain, but light, faint. The fear of sickness has faded, and a breathless fatigue rises instead. I climb no more than ten paces before stopping again, heaving for air. The merest extra effort – to mount a ledge or overstep a stone – exacts this gasping price. I wait for the panicky breathlessness of my avalanche ascent to return, but it does not. I fix my eyes on the ground beneath me, patterned with a dull glitter of snow. My feet march like somebody else's. I steer them from rock to rock. They climb past boulders newly dressed in votive clothes, and oxygen canisters discarded in the clefts. A tuft of hair – human or yak – drifts at my ankles. A horse's skull shines in the snow.

People die here. Many think it safer to ride than to walk. Kawaguchi, racked by headaches, and even Sven Hedin ascended the pass on yaks. The accident-prone Swami Hamsa was almost swept to his death in an avalanche. Others drowned in the freezing river below Drira Phuk, before a new bridge was built in 1986. The Hindu dead are routinely flown back to India, but others remain on the mountain.

Hedin noticed a corpse tumbled into a crevice like a bunch of rags, and recent pilgrims stumbled on the eviscerated torso of a girl.

Even the Tibetans falter sometimes, and fall forward on the boulders, the women's dark, bright-ringed hands clenching the stone. The Indians ride ashen-faced on their ponies, their mouths masked. Out of the pass ahead an ice-cold wind is blowing. Our breath rasps with weakness or prayer. It dies among the clink and shuffle of hooves and boots. I stop to write these notes, crouched on my knees. My fingers have gone numb, my handwriting broken. Now, as I try to read it, I see only words blurring like cuneiform into the damp from sleet or streaming nostrils. A pilgrim beside me cries out something, but whatever meaning I understood has faded illegibly from the page. So has my worry about Iswor, gone fast ahead. The wider landscape too – the shapes of surrounding peaks – has wandered into gibberish.

The sage Gotsampa, pioneering the kora, became the first to ascend the pass. After straying along the Secret Path of the Dakinis, he was lured here by a posse of twenty-one blue wolves. As he followed them in wonder they dissolved one into another until only a single beast was left, which disappeared into the rock face on the crown of the pass. Then the hermit knew that he had been guided by a vision of the twenty-one Taras, emanations of the goddess of compassion. This was her hill of salvation. Beyond it the way plunges for over a thousand feet into the valley. But here, at the 18,600-foot zenith of the kora, in a moment of blinding transition, pilgrims might pass into purity at the axis of the world.

Now hoarse cries sound above us in the wind, and a

hillock of brilliant colour bursts from the gap above. I climb on a wave of relief. The slopes ease apart under a porcelain sky. A few minutes later I am walking through a blaze of prayer flags. They are festooned so thick on everything around that only at their top does the double summit of the boulder sacred to Tara – the Flaming Rock – break free in a surge of granite. The poles from which the flags once flew have long crashed under their weight before the gales that fly through the pass, leaving this formless ocean of parched and vivid pennants heaped on boulders all around. Pilgrims trying to circumambulate the sacred stone flounder among ropes and shrouded rocks. Only here and there, if you part the brilliant curtain from the stone, do you glimpse the mantras blazoned in crimson and yellow, with money glued by butter to the surface, or hanks of hair, even people's teeth. Stubbornly I plunge across the boulders through this undergrowth. My feet snag among thrown-off clothes, shoes, dishes and animal skulls lying on half-melted ice. But an infectious victory is in the air.

Exhausted pilgrims sit in groups. They feast on tea and roasted barley. Others tear aside the flags to touch their palms and foreheads to the rock. A circle of men crouch in prayer that sounds like purring cats. Two monks sit facing one another in silence, and Hindu pilgrims are passing round their *prasada* sweets in dazed celebration. From time to time a new arrival breaks into a joyous shout. Prayer leaves scatter in the air and blow away. And once a pair of shamans, their torn robes fringed in scarlet and gold, their hair flying wild, leap up to hurl *tsampa* into the wind, and cry on and on: *'Lha-so-so-so! Lha-so-so!'* Victory to the gods!

I slump between their groups, washed in their happiness. Among these stark precipices the artificial riot of flags throws up an almost violent wave of prayer, touching and defiant. Even the farther outcrops are draped in banners where the pawprint left in the rock by Gotsampa's wolf shows clear to the eye of faith.

The twenty-one dissolving wolves proclaim the goddess of the place. To the Tibetans this protean deity is Drolma, the goddess of liberation, and it is she who forgives their sins and returns them newly pure to the world below. In her favourite guises as the Green and the White Tara, the divinities of motherhood and action, she sits on a throne of lotus and moon, and sometimes extends one leg in readiness to act. But her body may go through rainbow colours, and as the twenty-one Taras (who look almost identical in fresco) she diffuses into multiple benevolence, and she has the power to descend unscathed into hell. Above all she is the deity of pity, born from the tears of Avalokitesvara, the bodhisattva of compassion, as he wept at his powerlessness to comfort all living things. Call on her name, evoke her mandala, and she will fly in to the rescue. Her statues speak. She is the mother of the Tibetan people, and has moved through their mortal history as a pious queen or consort, so that illiterate pilgrims know her petition, which is being breathed against her prayer-hung rock as I watch.

It is the custom to leave some object on Drolma's pass, and to take something else away. Iswor, who is waiting for me, has brought a string of prayer flags from Darchen, and together we stretch them among the others. But he is feeling vaguely ill again. Under the scarf-swathed cap, the dark glasses, the glisten of sun cream, I imagine his face too pale. He wants to go down fast, but is ashamed to abandon me. He carries a heavy pack; I, almost nothing. I urge him away.

For a while I linger, reluctant to leave, although the sun has clouded. Other pilgrims are starting to trickle away. I wait, as if something might happen. But there is only the sandpaper wind and the paling sky. The air is thinner than any I have sensed. The euphoria of those around me lifts into momentary chanting that touches me like a benign contagion.

Deep in one pocket I find the sandalwood incense-sticks that Tashi had given me to burn for him on the pass. He had said: 'I think I will never reach there myself. But you will have gone for me.'

I scrutinise the packet in the hardening wind. It reads: 'Not only to please the Buddhas and Guardian divinities, but also to satiate the ordinary beings from the six realms and pacify demons and obstacle makers (sandalwood and secret substances).'

I have forgotten to bring matches, but a fervent youth – prayer beads in one hand, a camera in the other – offers me his cigarette lighter. After a long time I ignite a sheaf and shelter it among some flags. I call up Tashi's memory in the teeth of the wind. Then I start down.

One mile and 1,400 near-vertical feet to the valley below, and I am starting too late for comfort. The trail plummets over flint-sharp rocks, down the spine of a precipitous ridge with no end in sight, nothing to soften the grey wreckage underfoot, no hint of grass or flower. The path is too steep for yaks, and the ponies go riderless.

But almost at once the tarn of Gaurikund – among the highest lakes in the world – appears in a basin just below. Dark under its cliffs, ringed by the cloudy jade of softening ice, its centre is still pure snow, and the way down to it so arduous that few pilgrims attempt it. Buddhists call it the Lake of Mercy. It is the bathing pool of the sky-dancers, and of the goddess Parvati, wife of Shiva, who seduced him by her ablutions. Only in late summer do hardy pilgrims clamber down to collect the water, and pour it over their heads as a freezing baptism.

I pass a fresh sari, beautiful in purple and gold, discarded on the path. Nearby a sad-faced Hindu lies propped among rocks, gazing at the lake. He calls out to me: 'How far is it to the valley? How many hours?'

I hazard a guess. He is an Indian from Malaysia, and has never seen anywhere like this. 'I didn't understand, I thought it would be easy. Yet here I am.' He looks finished. 'But the others have gone.'

'Gone where?'

'Only seven of our group made it, out of twenty-three.'

'But you're over the hardest now.'

'We were told that if we bathed in Manasarovar, and finished the *parikrama* of Kailas, everything would be all right . . .'

'That you would gain merit? Perhaps moksha?' This is the Hindu nirvana.

'Perhaps.' But the word comes so drained, so disheartened, that it seems irrelevant. It is the long descent ahead that obsesses him. 'The other six have gone in front of me.' He touches my arm. 'Will there be horses at the bottom?'

'Yes, there will be horses.' I am guessing again. 'And the way will be level.' That much I know. 'It's a river valley. Beautiful.'

He wavers to his feet as I leave him. It is long before dusk, but a deep, sunless cold is settling in. The knee-jarring descent is still dotted with pilgrims. They clasp one another's hands as they go, still praying, and even now stop to touch their fingers to rocks dented by Milarepa's feet — stones smeared with cotton threads and yak butter — or add a pebble to a cairn. I glimpse Iswor, two hundred feet below me, waiting, and blunder down among loosened shale. A flotsam of empty cans and cigarette cartons strews the way, as if even litter becomes holy here. On either side the slopes sink in diagonal blades towards the Lham-chu valley, while the skyline shatters into crags. High to our right a black peak named the Axe of Karma threatens the sky, but not (it is said) the pilgrim walking in Tara's grace.

I come at last into a valley soft with evening sun. Beyond an isolated rock imprinted by the Buddha, the Lham river flows through level grasslands, and nomad horses tinkle on its far side. I have eight miles to go, but the way is easy beside sliding rivulets, shielded by mountains converted to Buddhism long ago. From another prostration platform the eastern tip of Kailas momentarily breaks into view, while to my left gleams the mountain of the Medicine Buddha, whose slopes are spread with healing herbs and minerals.

The sun has set by the time I reach camp. A few stars are out, and the meadows under Zutrul Phuk monastery, the Cave of Miracles, are quiet with sleeping yaks and foreign tents. Ram, who has glided ahead of us all day, augments our iron rations with warming soup. We sit silent together, while the night cold waits outside. Now that the pass is behind us, we all seem drained. We spread our sleeping bags on the hard earth as if its stones were velvet. For a while I write notes by torchlight, trying to recall the colour of pilgrims' clothes, the texture of rocks on the pass. But my fingers are stiff with cold, and I soon give up. In the minutes before sleep, a shadowy melancholy descends: the bewilderment when something long awaited has gone.

A wan light has broken around the tent. I have slept only fitfully. Outside, the Saga Dawa moon still hangs in the dawn, a leftover ghost above the misted valley. Beside our tent a rivulet of the Lham-chu crackles through ice-splinters; but I notice for the first time the tint of yellow shrubs familiar from Nepal trickling back between the rocks, like the return of old life.

The monastery crouches under the wind-shattered terraces that pour down from Kailas to the west. Its walls are rough-built and low, lined by small, regular windows like the gun ports of a galleon. Its history, like that of all these Kagyu outposts, is one of mixed marvel and obscurity. Founded in the 1220s, yet so poor a century ago that only a single caretaker lived here, it was razed in the Cultural Revolution, then rebuilt in 1983 as this mud-brick redoubt.

Shivering in its temple at dawn, I pass now-familiar figures – Avalokitesvara, Amitabha, Padmasambhava – seated like inquisitors in their jade-green haloes, until I reach the cave of miracles. This too is familiar: a rocky overhang, no more, where the poet-sage Milarepa meditated and sang.

The imprinted stones laid on its altar preserve the passage of other saints and hermits, even the hoofprint of the steed of King Gesar of Ling. But its treasure in this place of his power is the figure of Milarepa. The original statue, it is said, was shaped from the saint's own blood and excrement by a tantric disciple, the Divine Madman of Tsang, but this, if it ever existed, has gone. Instead another, bronze Milarepa sits on his stone altar. Of all bodhisattvas, his statues are the easiest to recognise, for he cups his right hand to his ear, listening to the whisper of the sky-dancers, perhaps, or to his own singing.

His life story, recited to a disciple before his death in 1135, is one of black magic and self-violence, rapt attachments and their sundering, ascetic tribulation and ecstasy, all told with the intimacy, even charm, of a first-person narrative that has endeared Milarepa to his people for centuries. In fact this autobiography, together with most of Milarepa's songs, was written by a scholar 400 years after the life it recalled; but whatever its source, it casts Milarepa in a role of human poignancy.

His is a tale of fearful penitence for the murderous crimes of his youth inspired by a vengeful mother, whom he loved. For years he served the grim teacher Marpa, who put him through Sisyphean torments before he was shriven. When he returned to his former home he found the house derelict in the moonlight, shunned by villagers who still feared his memory. Inside he came upon a mound of rags and bones that he realised with horror had once been his mother, and on this he rested his head for seven days, practising the transience of all things.

For years he lived as a hermit, near-naked in isolated caves. He ate only nettles, so that in legend his skin turned green. His sister, who at last discovered him, called him a human caterpillar. In the end his appearance became so terrifying that people fled on sight of him. But he himself felt refined to pure spirit. Often he would break into extempore song. Slowly his life and his teaching attracted a core of disciples, before he died at the age of eighty-three, poisoned by a jealous rival. His life and poetry, whoever composed them, turned him into Tibet's transcendent saint, so that long after his death a devotee claimed simply: 'People could tread on him, use him as a road, as earth; he would always be there.'

Around Kailas, Milarepa became the agent by which Buddhism supplanted the Bon, and his mythic deeds pervade the mountain. A Bon magician became the victim of Milarepa's greater magic, and the rocks of their contest – Milarepa pulling Bonchung round the kora clockwise – had haunted our way. In a final contest the Bon magician challenged the Buddhist mystic to reach the summit of Kailas before him, and started to fly there on his shaman's drum. But Milarepa, travelling on a sunbeam, alighted first, and the magician's drum, bouncing down the mountain's south face, left the scars that mark it still. In an act of reconciliation, Milarepa gave the ousted faith another mountain, where its faithful still circle anticlockwise: the same mountain that comforted the old Bon lama in Kathmandu, and that rises snowlit over Manasarovar's northern shore.

The Cave of Miracles, so dark that I can barely see, is rife with Milarepa's magic. The thrust of his hands and shoulders dimples the rock ceiling where he lifted it up, and his footprint is revered on the roof above, where he tamped the ceiling down. Even his stone trident is here, although fractured by Red Guards, and a knob of rock that protects those who caress it.

An attendant monk points to fingerprints in the soot-glazed ceiling. They come cold to my touch. Milarepa shoved the living rock about to create a temperate cave. Or so the monk says. The spiritual ordeal in the saint's tale is barely imaginable, but its human detail is gently moving: how mice are nesting on the shelves of his childhood home; how his fiancée wonderingly leaves him. On his fleeting homecoming the sale of his half-decayed books pays for the prayers for his mother's transmigrating soul. These mildewed tomes are his last possession, and of these he rids himself. He leaves the village clutching his mother's bones between his clothing and his chest, like the very signature of transience – his own and hers. What other comfort was there for the bereaved? Only what the limits of human awareness told him: that everything, all appearances, were mistaken.

I leave money for his butter lamps before I go, and watch them ignite under the monk's hands.

Behind the monastery the cliffs are riddled with abandoned caves where the dawn light leaks over empty hearths and meditation platforms. All along the slopes, thousands of mani stones and carved boulders fire batteries of prayer across the valley. We turn to leave. The river flows full and blue now, bending south-west. Iswor is buoyant again, his head clear, while I go dreamily, as if days of fatigue were catching up.

The path lifts high over the river now and winds above a canyon daubed purple and black: the blood of the Devil's demon yak, it is said, slaughtered by Gesar of Ling. We tramp dazedly above, through scrub and russet shale, staring down precipices of harlequin oddness. Through this palette two pilgrims are moving forward like caterpillars, prostrating on the stones, rising again, their padded hands lifted praying, falling. Their faces are black and muffled: two women, young, tired. One still mumbles prayers with each prostration, the other mews like a kitten. The dust of passing ponies closes their eyes.

I overtake them cautiously, as if skirting some private rite, although they lift their faces and smile. Within an hour I have crested the canyon path, and there opens out beyond me the remembered peace of the Barga plain. Beneath us the diffused headwaters of the Sutlej river are seeping from the slopes a thousand miles before it joins the Indus, and the sky is static with clouds. The kora is closing now, turning along the southern hills of Kailas. Forty miles away, clear across the plateau, the white upheaval of Gurla Mandhata appears, with Rakshas Tal, the demon lake, stretched indigo below, and close at hand a path leads under the last foothills, where pilgrims are walking home.

INDEX

Index

Chenresig (Buddhist god), 49, 65,
206
Cherkip *see* Serkyi Cherkip
China: bans pilgrimages to Kailas,
7; Cultural Revolution, 7, 114,
117, 121, 184, 192, 214; invades
Tibet (1959), 32, 43, 46, 82; and
power of Mount Kailas, 34;
Khampa resistance to, 79; closes
Tibet's borders, 85; attacked by
medieval Tibetan warriors, 88;
road-building in Tibet, 91, 95;
immigration officials in Tibet,
108; destruction and persecution in Tibet, 111, 114, 121, 134,
170, 214, 217; troops in Tibet,
146, 170, 217; soldiers at Mount
Kailas, 148–9, 157–8, 160; Red
Guards, 170
Chiu monastery, 123–5, 127–8
Choku monastery, 170–4
chortens, 71, 166–7
Christianity: missionaries in Tibet,
99, 102, 164; and Tibetan Buddhism, 102–3

dakinis, 153, 108, 195–6; *see also*
sky-dancers
Dakshinkali valley, 67–8
Dalai Lama: flight from Tibet, 32–
3, 106; and reincarnation, 45,
49; and hidden Shambala, 82;
status, 102; Chinese hostility to,
109
Damding Donkhang, 185
Darchen, Tibet, 144–6
dead, the: disposal in Tibet,
150–2, 154; and mountain path,
184–5; and Vajra Yogini burial

ground, 195–7; and reincarna-
tion, 201
death: denied by Hindus, 141–2;
ritual and experience
of, 198–202; *see also Tibetan
Book of the Dead, The*
delok (returned from dead), 202
Demchog (god), 137, 150, 158–9,
175, 193–4
Deng Xiaoping, 111
Desideri, Ippolito, SJ, 98–9, 129,
143
Dharamsala, 60
Dharapuri, 93
Dhaulagiri (mountain), 1
Doyle, Sir Arthur Conan, 31
Drachom Ngagye Durtro, 150
Drira Phuk Gompa (Monastery of
the Cave of the Yak Horns),
186–7, 195
Drokpa people (Tibet), 110, 157
Drolma (Buddhist goddess), 49, 53,
210
Drolma-la river, 191, 195, 205
Durtros, 150, 152, 154

Ellora (temple, India), 139
Everest, Mount, 1

Flaming Rock (sacred stone), 209

Ganga Chu river, 128
Gandhi, Mohandas Karamchand
(Mahatma), 141
Ganges river: source, 5, 100, 128;
course, 129
Gaurikund (tarn), 212
Gekko (Bon deity), 177
Gelugpa (Buddhist sect), 104

Index

Index

About the author

About the book

Insights,
Interviews
& More . . .

Read on

Meet Colin Thubron

© Colin McPherson

I HAVE WANTED TO WRITE since childhood. My mother must have had something to do with this. She came from the family of John Dryden, the first poet laureate of England, and encouraged my juvenile poetry. My father was an army officer, and was American on his mother's side, a descendant of Samuel Morse, inventor of the Morse code.

I had a privileged childhood, growing up in my parents' rural home in southeast England. But the British custom of sending children away to boarding school from the age of seven made for a hard, early lesson in self-sufficiency. These were the immediate postwar years (I was born in 1939), and life in Britain was still somber. But when I was eight my father was posted to Washington and Ottawa for four years, and the excitement of this new world, with the vastness of the North American landscapes, came like a revelation to a boy from war-drab England, and perhaps planted the first seeds of fascination with places abroad.

In 1953 I went to Eton, a school that encouraged independence, and typically excelled in English and history, and failed at mathematics. By the time I left, in 1957, I knew only that I wanted to write. I went into publishing, spending four years with Hutchinson as a trainee, then assistant editor. For a year and a half afterwards my love of travel took me abroad making freelance documentaries for BBC television in Turkey, Morocco and Japan. This was followed by a brief return to publishing in New York (1964–1965) with Macmillan Publishers, as a production editor.

In late 1965 I took the plunge into full-time writing, and settled with an Arab family in Damascus to start my first travel book. *Mirror to Damascus* was published in 1967, and was successful enough to open a future. Soon afterwards I traveled on foot through Lebanon for *The Hills of Adonis* (1968) and settled in Jerusalem in the year after the Six-Day War for *Jerusalem* (1969).

But I had always hankered after writing novels, and, after a grim ▶

66 In late 1965 I took the plunge into full-time writing, and settled with an Arab family in Damascus to start my first travel book. 99

3

apprenticeship with failed ideas, produced *The God in the Mountain* (1977), set in Cyprus, and a travel book on the island, *Journey into Cyprus* (1975). This was followed by a second novel, *Emperor*, a multifaceted story of the conversion of Constantine, and *A Cruel Madness* (winner of the Silver Pen Award in Britain), set in a mental hospital.

At that time my travel books had all been about geographically small places. Then, in 1978, something changed: a motor accident, a fractured spine, and some emotional sadness started a new direction. I decided to learn Russian and take a car into the Soviet Union, whose gray unchangingness (this was Brezhnev's time) made it an unlikely subject for a successful travel book. But I went in summer, spending the nights in student-run camps, and was only harassed by the KGB in my last weeks. The resulting book, *Among the Russians* (published in the United States as *Where Nights Are Longest*) coincided with a surge of popularity for the travel book genre in Britain, and gave me financial security.

In 1985, after studying Mandarin, I traveled through China at a time when the country was cautiously opening its doors. The resulting *Behind the Wall: A Journey Through China* won the Hawthornden Prize and the Thomas Cook Travel Book Award, and was followed, in 1994, by a venture into the newly emerged Muslim republics of the broken-up Soviet Union for *The Lost*

Heart of Asia. A long journey through the now-accessible Russian heartland produced *In Siberia* in 1999.

Throughout the past thirty years I have alternated travel books with novels. The two genres are often reactions against one another. The novels are introverted and intense— one, for instance, set in a mental hospital, another in a prison, another in an amnesiac's brain. I have published successively *Falling* (1989), *Turning Back the Sun* (1991), *Distance* (1996) and *To the Last City* (2002). These are stark, short tales, sometimes autobiographical in feeling, but not in plot.

The travel books, on the contrary, stem from a fascination with the outer world, often distant and little-known. My concentration on the lands of the old Soviet Union, on China, and on Islam reflected at first a romantic obsession with the great civilisations of Asia. But more recently, after *Among the Russians*, the books have grappled with the darker concerns and fears of my generation.

> " Throughout the past thirty years I have alternated travel books with novels. The two genres are often reactions against one another. "

Q&A: *Publishers Weekly* Talks with Colin Thubron

Tibet: A Region in the Mind

With his mother's death the catalyst, Colin Thubron travels *To a Mountain in Tibet* (Reviews, Dec. 13) to one of the holiest Hindu sites.

You describe Tibet as "less a country than a region in the mind," particularly for Western visitors. Do you think it will always have this mystique for Westerners?

Tibet is so remote, so harsh, and its culture so strange to us, that I think the mystique will endure for a long time. But in a sense, the flight of the Dalai Lama in 1959 plucked out the country's heart. No regime is more antithetic to Tibet than the drab materialism of China, whose grip on the country grows ever tighter. Beijing, at best, will aspire to turn the Tibetan religious world into a tourist theme park. It is in the Tibetan diaspora—among the monks who fled to the West—that the mystique may most forcibly endure. But over here this legacy is threatened by the insidious demands of a very different culture: by a focus less on Buddhism's exacting mystical practices than on Buddhism as a therapy.

A Buddhist abbot you met typified the struggles you faced: he focused on "spiritual continuance" while you were "overborne with individual death." Were you ever able to reconcile the two?

I wish I could answer yes to this—it would make a happier narrative. But it wasn't so. After the death of the last of my family, I was travelling to a sacred object—a mountain—in a spirit of pilgrimage, but the mountain was holy only to others and I am agnostic. Nor does the Buddhist hereafter offer much consolation. It promises the endurance of nothing recognizable: no memory, nothing beloved or even individual. Its concern is with karma. So, no, there was no reconciliation, and no profound comfort. There was only the feeling of having marked the passage of my family by making a journey and placing it in this book.

You're no stranger to extended travels in foreign countries. Did your preparation for this trip differ from previous projects?

I'm an avid researcher—it's normally part of the fun. The research on *Shadow of the Silk Road*, as for many of my books, was much concerned with studying languages. I have wrestled with Russian and Mandarin Chinese for half my life, and both were necessary for the *Silk Road*. (Russian is still the lingua franca for the older generation in Central Asia.) But for Tibet I drew the line. The language is infernally difficult, and I never attempted it. My research ▶

7

Q&A: *Publishers Weekly* Talks with Colin Thubron *(continued)*

was concentrated on trying to understand Tibetan Buddhism— an arcane and fascinating branch of the faith.

Even though the question of why you chose to climb Mount Kailas is a complex one, did the experience bring you any sense of peace?

Nothing clear-cut. But it did put a space between me and the immediate past, and this seemed necessary to me. It is a wise culture, I think, which supplies rituals for marking bereavement. Our own supplies these very little, and sometimes we have to invent them. ∽

—Jordan Foster

Have You Read?
More by Colin Thubron

SHADOW OF THE SILK ROAD

To travel the Silk Road, the greatest land route on earth, is to trace the passage not only of trade and armies but also of ideas, religions, and inventions. Making his way by local bus, truck, car, donkey cart, and camel, Colin Thubron covered some seven thousand miles in eight months—out of the heart of China into the mountains of Central Asia, across northern Afghanistan and the plains of Iran into Kurdish Turkey—and explored an ancient world in modern ferment.

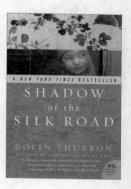

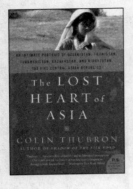

Read on

Have You Read? *(continued)*

THE LOST HEART OF ASIA

A land of enormous proportions, countless secrets, and incredible history, Central Asia—the heart of the great Mongol empire of Tamerlane, site of the legendary Silk Route and scene of Stalin's cruelest deportations—is a remote and fascinating region. Since the collapse of the Soviet Union and the emergence of newly independent republics, Central Asia—containing the magical cities of Bukhara and Samarkand, and terrain as diverse as the Kazakh steppes, the Kara-Kum desert, and the Pamir mountains—has been in a constant state of transition. *The Lost Heart of Asia* takes readers into the very heart of this little-visited, yet increasingly important region, delivering a rare and moving portrayal of a world in the midst of change.

"Thubron has a novelist's sensitivity and an historian's perception. One could not ask for a more rewarding travel companion through a little-known land."
—*Washington Post Book World*

As mysterious as it is beautiful, as
forbidding as it is populated with
warm-hearted people, Siberia is a land
few Westerners know, and even fewer
will ever visit. Traveling alone, by train,
boat, car, and on foot, Colin Thubron
traversed this vast territory, talking to
everyone he encountered about the state
of the country, whose natural resources
have been savagely exploited for decades;
a terrain tainted by nuclear waste but
filled with citizens who both welcomed
him and fed him—despite their own
tragic poverty. From Mongolia to the
Artic Circle, from Rasputin's village
in the west through tundra, taiga,
mountains, lakes, rivers, and finally
to a derelict Jewish community in the
country's far eastern reaches, Colin
Thubron penetrates a little-understood
part of the world in a way that no writer
ever has.

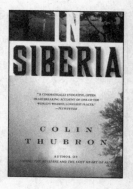

"Thubron's ability to see, feel, analyze,
to blend the present and the past, makes
In Siberia more than a travel book. His
keen eye, like a great photographer's,
sees more than an image; he captures
the essence of Siberia."

—*Chicago Tribune*

AMONG THE RUSSIANS

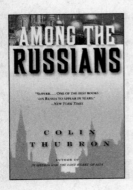

Here is a fresh perspective on the last tumultuous years of the Soviet Union and an exquisitely poetic travelogue. With a keen grasp of Russia's history, a deep appreciation for its architecture and iconography, and an inexhaustible enthusiasm for its people and its culture, Colin Thubron is the perfect guide to a country most of us will never know firsthand. Here, we can walk down western Russia's country roads, rest in its villages, and explore some of the most engaging cities in the world. Beautifully written and infinitely insightful, *Among the Russians* is vivid, compelling travel writing that will also appeal to readers of history and current events—and to anyone seeking connection with one of the world's most enigmatic cultures.

"Superb. . . . One of the best books on Russia to appear in years."
—*New York Times*

"Colin Thubron is an ideal guide. Well informed about icons, architecture, and history, he is also wonderfully articulate . . . especially in descriptive passages, the language becomes a grave and stately music."
—*Washington Post Book World*

Don't miss the next book by your favorite author. Sign up now for AuthorTracker by visiting www.AuthorTracker.com.